PULPIT AFLAME

PULPIT AFLAME

ESSAYS IN HONOR OF STEVEN J. LAWSON

edited by Joel R. Beeke and Dustin W. Benge

Reformation Heritage Books
Grand Rapids, Michigan

Pulpit Aflame
© 2016 by Dustin W. Benge

Reformation Heritage Books
2965 Leonard St. NE
Grand Rapids, MI 49525
616–977–0889 / Fax 616–285–3246
orders@heritagebooks.org
www.heritagebooks.org

All Scripture quotations, unless otherwise indicated, are taken from the New King James Version. Copyright © 1982 by Thomas Nelson, Inc. Used by permission. All rights reserved.

Printed in the United States of America
16 17 18 19 20 21/10 9 8 7 6 5 4 3 2 1

Library of Congress Cataloging-in-Publication Data

Names: Lawson, Steven J., honouree. | Beeke, Joel R., 1952- editor.
Title: Pulpit aflame : essays in honor of Steven J. Lawson / edited by Joel R. Beeke
    and Dustin W. Benge.
Description: Grand Rapids, Michigan : Reformation Heritage Books, 2016. |
    Includes bibliographical references.
Identifiers: LCCN 2016011139 (print) | LCCN 2016011475 (ebook) | ISBN
    9781601784650 (hardcover : alk. paper) | ISBN 9781601784667 (epub)
Subjects: LCSH: Preaching.
Classification: LCC BV4222 .P85 2016 (print) | LCC BV4222 (ebook) | DDC
    251—dc23
LC record available at http://lccn.loc.gov/2016011139

For additional Reformed literature, request a free book list from Reformation Heritage Books at the above regular or e-mail address.

Contents

Foreword

Ian Hamilton

From my earliest days as a young Christian in Glasgow, I have been vastly privileged to be exposed to preaching that instructed me, stirred me, humbled me, challenged me, and sometimes plunged me into the depths, but then lifted me up to the heights. I have sometimes marveled at the different personalities, temperaments, gifts, and backgrounds that marked those men whose preaching ministries God used to shape my life and ministry. There was nothing formulaic or monochrome about them. Each one of the men (and I have five particular men in mind) modeled Phillips Brooks's dictum that preaching is truth through personality. But while these men were so different in regard to their personalities, there were common features in their preaching that marked them out as men set apart by God to preach His Word.

First, before they were anything else, these preachers were men of God. What first deeply impressed me about these men was not their preaching, but their manifest godliness. Their preaching was simply an extension of who and what they were. There was a seamlessness between what these men were outside the pulpit and what they were in the pulpit. There was no artificiality, no "pulpit voice," no acting a part. In classical Greek society, the *hypokrites* was a play actor, someone who acted a part by wearing a mask. There was nothing these five men more excoriated than spiritual pretense. Their weak humanity shone through their preaching, and they allowed it to do so. You can be sure that where there is not heart holiness in the preacher, his words will sound hollow and lifeless, no matter how gilded with eloquence and orthodox theology.

Second, they were men committed to the systematic expository preaching of God's Word. Foundational to this commitment was the unshakable conviction that "all Scripture is given by inspiration of God, and is profitable for doctrine, for reproof, for correction, for instruction in righteousness, that the man of God may be complete, thoroughly equipped for every good work" (2 Tim. 3:16–17). Not *some* Scripture, not *most* Scripture, but *all* Scripture is necessary to complete or make perfect the man of God. Only as God's people are exposed to the length and breadth, height and depth of God's saving revelation will they truly grow up into Christ.

It is sadly true, however, that some men committed to the systematic, expository preaching of God's Word miss the wood for the trees. They are so intent on verse-by-verse exposition that they fail to grasp and pass on to others the big picture embedded in every paragraph of Scripture. That big picture is the grace and glory of God in Christ—promised, come, crucified, risen, ascended, reigning, and returning (this is what Martyn Lloyd-Jones epitomized in his verse-by-verse biblical expositions). This is why biblical and systematic theology are the necessary handmaidens of truly biblical, systematic, expository preaching.

Third, they were men committed to expository preaching that addressed both the minds and hearts of their hearers. Preaching seeks to address whole men and women in the totality of their humanity. Biblical preaching will necessarily seek to inform the mind and capture it with the compelling truth of God's Word. But no less will it seek to address and engage the affections of men and women. The religion of the Bible is deeply and ineradicably affectional. Jonathan Edwards was only too right when he said that "true religion, in great part, consists in holy affections." God is never content with orthodox confessions of faith. He seeks the love of our hearts and joyful delight suffusing our obedience.

Fourth, they were men who preached God's Word with a palpable zeal for God's glory. The first great concern of any preacher worthy of the name is a desire for God to be glorified in his ministerial labors. What gives preaching a luster that compels the attention of believers and unbelievers alike is the preacher's complete disinterest in commending himself.

Self-promotion is one of the sins that so scars modern evangelical Christianity. Celebrity preachers peddle the latest gimmick in developing self-worth, making man and not God in Christ the focus of their "preaching." The faithful, God-honoring preacher will be kept from such perversions because as he preaches the whole counsel of God, he comes to understand that even the salvation and sanctification of sinners is the proximate, not the ultimate, aim of a God-honoring preacher. The preacher's ultimate aim is the glory of the triune God: "For of Him and through Him and to Him are all things, to whom be glory forever. Amen" (Rom. 11:36).

Fifth, they were men who preached God's Word understanding that the Lord Jesus Christ is both the epicenter and omega point of God's saving revelation. As I sat under the varied ministries of these five men, I began to understand that no matter where you were in the Bible, Jesus Christ was in the foreground and actually never in the background. These biblical expositors relentlessly impressed on me that the whole Bible was an exposition of the first gospel promise (Gen. 3:15). It is therefore vastly significant that the risen Lord rebuked the two disciples on the road to Emmaus for being foolish and "slow of heart to believe in all that the prophets have spoken." He then, "beginning at Moses and all the Prophets…expounded to them in all the Scriptures the things concerning Himself" (Luke 24:25–27).

Sixth, they were men who preached God's Word passionately. I need to explain what I mean. I do not mean they preached loudly (though on occasion they did) or used particularly emotive language. I do mean that they preached out of the overflow of their hearts. There was an unmistakable and even compelling passion that pulsed through their preaching. I believe that each of these men exhibited in their lives the substance of John Calvin's motto: "Cor meum tibi offero Domine, prompte et sincere" (My heart I give to you, O Lord, promptly and sincerely). It is out of such heart devotion that God-honoring preaching flows.

I often found it remarkable that these men were so different in their personalities and temperaments. One was at heart shy. Another was outgoing. A third was deeply idiosyncratic. The fourth was elegant in style, with the most mellifluous voice. The fifth was deeply read and richly theological. But one thing united these five different men: they preached out of lives that loved Jesus Christ with adoring humility. When I think of systematic, expository preaching, I think of these men.

Seventh, they were men who preached God's Word *coram Deo* (before God's face). No man can begin to preach the gospel of God's grace in Christ who is more concerned not to offend men than to please and honor God. The divine calling to "preach the word in good times and in bad times" (2 Tim. 4:2, my translation) requires a boldness that is not of man. Faithful, God-sent, and not merely church-ordained men discover that the God who sent them gives them a boldness in preaching that is not merely a personality trait. The Lord Jesus Christ was "gentle and lowly in heart" (Matt. 11:29), and yet when He confronted hypocrisy and worse in God's church, He preached with devastating and penetrating power (read Matthew 23). You might be thinking, "But no mere preacher begins to approximate the Lord Jesus Christ." Indeed, and yet the Lord's humanity was a true humanity. He was upheld throughout His life and ministry by the Holy Spirit as the better-than-Adam Servant of the Lord (Isa. 42:1). By His ministry of replication, what the Holy Spirit first forged in the sinless life of Jesus He comes to reproduce in the lives of all believers, and not least in the lives of God's preaching servants.

It is not coincidental, at least to me, that these seven marks of God-honoring preaching indelibly mark the preaching ministry of Steven J. Lawson. Dr. Lawson has a passion for preaching that is infectiously engaging. He not only commends expository preaching but he also models it in his sermons, which are full of exegetical thoroughness, expositional clarity, applicatory incisiveness, and a passionate zeal for God's glory. The essays in this *Festschrift* are a testimonial to Steve's heart desire for God-glorifying and Christ-centered preaching. But, more importantly, they are a testimonial to the God of grace, who gives the church, in His love and mercy, men who will faithfully proclaim His saving grace in Christ, men who fear God and not man, men who preach out of the overflow of lives captive to the grace of the Lord Jesus Christ, the love of God, and the comfort of the Holy Spirit.

CHAPTER 1

Steven J. Lawson: Knowing the Man and His Message

Dustin W. Benge

On June 29, 2014, Steven J. Lawson stood in the pulpit of Christ Fellowship Baptist Church in Mobile, Alabama, for the final time. The atmosphere within these white walls and stained glass windows was heavy with heartfelt sadness. Many sitting in the congregation had heard Lawson preach every Lord's Day for almost twenty years.

Christ Fellowship is a church that had been birthed thirteen years earlier from the ashes of theological division and the spark of the bold proclamation of the truth. The men and women of this beloved church family had sat attentively Sunday after Sunday as Lawson had explained God's Word verse by verse, phrase by phrase, word by word. Under his expository ministry, many had come to know Christ and been baptized, while others had first become acquainted with the doctrines of grace. There were no adequate words of appreciation that anyone could muster on this "farewell Sunday."

Dressed in his signature crisp white shirt and narrow red and navy striped tie, Lawson, walking to the wooden pulpit, culminated his pastoral ministry, which had spanned several states over the past thirty years. With tear-filled eyes and a trembling voice, turning the pages in his Bible, Lawson said, "For one last time, I ask you to take God's Word and turn with me to the book of Philippians, chapter 4." He continued, "For those of you visiting today, I don't normally act this way. This is my last Sunday to be the pastor of this wonderful flock of people. You have become very dear to me, and I want to express to you my deep love and affection as we have spent significant time together. The title of my message is 'A Fitting Farewell.'"

Lawson then read the words of the apostle: "Therefore, my beloved brethren whom I long to see, my joy and crown, in this way stand firm in the Lord, my beloved" (Phil 4:1 NASB). This short verse encapsulated Paul's affection for the church at Philippi, and it also epitomized Lawson's heart at the close of one ministry chapter and the opening of another.

Early Years

Steven James Lawson was born in Oklahoma City, Oklahoma, on April 13, 1951. His father, J. W. (James Wilkes) Lawson, worked for the government in medicine and pharmaceutical testing and research. Later, he became professor of pharmacology and vice chairman of the Department of Medical Chemistry at the University of Tennessee. Lawson's mother, Betty, was an accomplished artist and honor student throughout her years in school. After Steven was born, Betty stayed at home to raise him and his two younger siblings, Shelley and Mark.

The Lawson family attended church every Sunday and viewed the Lord's Day as the high point of the week. Essentially, Sunday morning began Saturday night. Lawson's father oversaw a Saturday evening ritual in which he instructed his son to lay out his suit coat, tie, freshly pressed shirt, and trousers for the next morning. He was to expertly polish his shoes. At an early age, Lawson received the message loud and clear that worshiping the Lord was the most important thing going on in the life of his family, and it required a certain level of seriousness and discipline.

The Lawsons openly discussed Christian topics and Scripture in their home, for spiritual matters were highly regarded and to be taken seriously. Both of Lawson's parents lived out the virtues of a godly life before their children and in their daily work. Lawson recalls that his father "was the most principled man I have ever known. His personal integrity and honesty were distinguishing marks of his life."

Lawson came to faith in Christ at an early age through the faithful witness of his parents. As a young boy, he listened each night as his father read Bible stories to him before bed. These stories began to plant seeds of gospel truth within his heart, which eventually brought conviction of sin and then later blossomed into salvation. In a recent interview, Lawson recalled, "When my father explained that Christ had suffered divine judgment upon the cross in the place of sinners like me, this was extraordinarily good news. By God's grace, I put my faith in Jesus Christ."

The Lawson family moved quite often due to J. W.'s position with the government, from New Jersey, where young Steven developed a love for Yankee baseball; to Fort Worth, Texas, where he became a diehard Dallas Cowboys fan; and then finally settling down in Memphis, Tennessee. Lawson entered his teen years attending White Station High School, where he discovered his love of sports. Throughout his adolescence, he grew to be an excellent athlete, enjoying baseball, basketball, track, and football. To the chagrin of his family, who held success in academics as the pinnacle of human achievement, he gave priority to his sports activities.

Lawson remembers his years playing football and participating in "two-a-days," a period of grueling preseason workouts in the blazing heat of summer. His high school team traveled south to Greenwood, Mississippi, for an entire week of two-a-days to prepare for a season they hoped would be victory filled. Lawson ate, breathed, and slept football during his high school days, which culminated in a football scholarship to Texas Tech University in Lubbock, Texas, after his graduation in 1969.

Calling into Ministry

Entering college, Lawson remained faithful to Christ, attending church, reading the Scriptures, and growing in his faith. During his first three years of college, he began several youth ministries for high school students. These ministries grew and were unusually blessed by God. Under his teaching, he saw several young people brought to faith in Christ.

While a freshman in college, Lawson had the experience of proclaiming God's Word for the first time. He was asked by the Fellowship of Christian Athletes to give his testimony of personal faith in Christ in Fluvana, Texas. The pastor who introduced him, however, told the small congregation that Lawson was going to bring the morning sermon. Though he admits he was terrified of public speaking at only eighteen years old, he found this initial experience of standing before a congregation with an open Bible exhilarating. This time served as the foundation upon which he would later stand as he surrendered to God's calling to preach. The drive and desire to stand and explain God's Word grew stronger as the years passed.

As Lawson began to realize he couldn't play football for the rest of his life, he grew increasingly miserable with his uncertain career path as God's call upon his life became clearer. Striving to find peace, he worked in politics, banking, and other ventures for a short time, but nothing satisfied this growing, insatiable desire to preach God's Word. He graduated from Texas Tech in 1973 with a bachelor of business administration degree and then entered the law school of Texas Tech, but never graduated. While studying law, Lawson began to realize the law he was learning often changed by the time exams were given, but God's laws never change and are forever fixed in eternity.

Dropping out of law school, he moved back to his family home in Memphis, taking a job at the First Tennessee Bank.

Providentially, during this uncertain time of searching for satisfaction, he sat under the powerful biblical preaching of Dr. Adrian Rogers at Bellevue Baptist Church in Memphis. Sunday after Sunday, he heard this man of God stand to preach. Lawson recounts that he was "blown away" by what he heard. He remembers, "I had never heard anyone handle the Scripture as he did. He became a living incarnation before my eyes of what was in my heart that I wanted to do." After much soul searching and agonizing prayer, he relinquished his life to preach the Word of God, to minister to His people, and to win the lost to Him.

Seminary and Family

In the mid-1970s, after surrendering his life to gospel ministry, Lawson loaded everything into the backseat of a small Volkswagen Bug and drove to seminary with a mere one hundred dollars in his pocket. His first experience was at Southwestern Seminary. During these turbulent liberal years within the Southern Baptist Convention, Lawson was immediately told not to cause trouble; he was suspect since he was "from Adrian Rogers's church." Rogers had built his ministry upon the inerrancy and infallibility of Scripture. Lawson was quickly told that Southwestern did not hold to such doctrine. With strong conviction in his heart for the truth of God's Word, he left Southwestern and transferred to Dallas Theological Seminary, from which he graduated in 1980 with his master of theology degree.

Lawson recognizes several professors at Dallas who invested in his life and made a large impact upon his preaching and future ministry. Haddon W. Robinson and Duane Litfin, who taught expository preaching, were responsible for key lessons he would never forget. Other professors at Dallas, men like Howard Hendricks, J. Dwight Pentecost, John Hannah, Stanley Toussaint, and Roy Zuck left their imprint upon Lawson during these years of theological training.

In the fall of 1979, during his last year at Dallas Seminary, Lawson meet Anne Crowell, who had recently moved to Dallas to be on the staff of Campus Crusade for Christ at Southern Methodist University. The Sunday they met, Lawson had just finished teaching a class of two hundred singles in the basement of Highland Park Presbyterian Church. Anne's former fiancé, who was traveling through town, invited Lawson to go to lunch with him, Anne, and Anne's roommate, who was very taken with Lawson's preaching. Even though

Lawson had never met any of them, he agreed to go. After their three-hour lunch, Anne and her roommate began to attend Lawson's weekly Bible study.

In January 1980, after turning in his ThM thesis, Lawson asked Anne if she would like to go with him to hear Adrian Rogers preach at a conference in Fort Worth. He has often recounted that if Anne had not liked Rogers, this would have been their only date. But her response was positive, and by May they were discussing marriage. Shortly after, Lawson asked Anne's father for her hand in marriage, to which he responded, "Son, you first need to get a job!"

Lawson accepted a position at the first church that contacted him, University Baptist Church in Fayetteville, Arkansas, where he became the collegiate pastor. Having fulfilled Anne's father's wishes, Lawson proposed to her by a small creek on the grounds of Highland Park Presbyterian Church.

He and Anne were married on April 18, 1981, in Asheville, North Carolina, near the Crowell summer home. In August 1981, Lawson was called to be the senior pastor of The Bible Church of Little Rock in Little Rock, Arkansas. During their fourteen years in Little Rock, he and Anne welcomed four children into their family. Their first two children, twins Andrew and James, were born on March 15, 1983; a daughter, Grace Anne, was delivered on April 20, 1987; and their youngest son, John, was born October 15, 1990.

Lawson's pastorate at The Bible Church of Little Rock established him as a strong expository preacher. Week after week, he practiced the skills of sermon preparation and delivery. During this time, he also decided to continue his education from a distance at Reformed Theological Seminary (RTS) in Jackson, Mississippi.

Lawson attended Reformed Seminary for the single purpose of being able to sit under the teaching of R. C. Sproul. He comments, "Dr. Sproul instructed me in the finer points of communication. Every one of his classes was filled with his passion to convey the truth of Scripture and still remains fresh and memorable in my mind." On May 18, 1990, he graduated from RTS with his doctorate in ministry degree.

Ministry in Alabama

In spring 1995, Lawson's family moved to Mobile, Alabama, where he had accepted the senior pastor position at Dauphin Way Baptist Church. Founded in 1904, Dauphin Way had become one of the largest churches on the Gulf Coast, with a prestigious list of previous pastors—kind of a "Who's Who" in the Southern Baptist Convention. Lawson accepted the call in the great hope that he could continue what he had dedicated his life to—verse-by-verse exposition.

After only a few years, however, Lawson began to experience difficulty at Dauphin Way after several in leadership and in the congregation began to disagree with his preaching on the doctrines of grace. He sought much guidance from his mentor and friend John MacArthur, but the two of them saw no solution to the problems of Dauphin Way except resignation. After heart-wrenching agony and prayer, he resigned his pastorate in January 2003. Upon his resignation almost half the congregation, with great affection for God's Word and for Lawson's expository ministry, decided also to leave the church.

The next Sunday found the Lawson family and hundreds of others without a place to worship. Lawson received a call to meet with the divided congregation and preach to them. He agreed, and out of these ashes of theological division emerged Christ Fellowship Baptist Church. Christ Fellowship was the pulpit that would see his greatest ministry, hear his most in-depth sermons, and become the crown of his pastoral ministry.

In the years that followed, Lawson took his passionate verse-by-verse expositional ministry to various conference venues and pulpits around the world. In October 2012, after consulting with many mentors and pastoral colleagues, he ventured out in faith to found OnePassion Ministries, an extension of his preaching ministry, to be based in Dallas.

OnePassion was founded to ignite a supreme passion for God and His glory in all people throughout the world. The intentional focus of OnePassion is to impart the knowledge of the truth by equipping pastors and church leaders, strengthening believers in all walks of life, and spreading the gospel of Jesus Christ around the world. Through OnePassion, Lawson is building a ministry platform to enflame hearts with an all-consuming desire for Jesus Christ and His gospel.

Worldwide Ministry

Prior to the launch of OnePassion, R. C. Sproul invited Lawson to become a teaching fellow at Ligonier Ministries in 2009. From his seminary days at Reformed Theological Seminary, he had always recognized Sproul as a mentor in theological training and preaching and was now happy to join him in ministry. Ligonier Ministries has provided Lawson with tremendous opportunities to write books, preach at conferences, and train men in preaching through the newly founded Institute for Expository Preaching.

In addition, in 2015, after Lawson had taught for several years at the Master's Seminary in Sun Valley, California, John MacArthur invited him to oversee the seminary's doctorate of ministry program in the area of expository preaching. Under Lawson's guidance, this program has transformed into one of the best places in the world for men to prepare for pulpit ministry.

Though Lawson is dedicated to instructing other preachers in biblical exposition, he is also committed to preaching to all segments of the international church. His bold preaching has taken him around the world, from Russia, Ukraine, Scotland, Wales, England, Ireland, and Germany to Japan, New Zealand, Switzerland, Italy, and South Africa. In addition, his sermons are posted online and listened to in all fifty states and numerous countries. Many who have never seen him have heard his voice and learned from his faithful proclamation of God's Word.

Lawson's sermons and the overflow of his diligent study and biblical preaching have been preserved in writing as well. He has authored more than twenty books, including biblical commentaries, books on Christian living, and surveys of church history and historical theology. He is the series editor of the Long Line of Godly Men biographies, published by Reformation Trust, and the executive editor of *Expositor* magazine, which features timely articles from leading expositors written for the instruction and nurturing of the coming generation of biblical preachers.

Biblically Driven

From the early days of his ministry, Lawson has been wholly committed to the sufficiency of Scripture. This commitment has fueled and driven everything he has preached for the past thirty years. From his time at seminary during the turbulent liberal days of the Southern Baptist Convention, he has been devoted to proclaiming the truth of God's Word.

Lawson recognizes a departure from the doctrine of the sufficiency of Scripture in the twentieth-century church. This departure is nowhere more clearly seen than in the evangelical pulpit. As he notes, "The content of preaching is becoming increasingly man-centered and overrun with heavy doses of cultural wisdom, therapeutic advice, psycho-babble, secular pragmatism, and political agendas, all mixed together with a barrage of personal anecdotes."[1] This departure from a firm belief in the sufficiency of Scripture

1. Steven J. Lawson, "The Sufficiency of Scripture in Preaching," *Expositor* 1 (September/October, 2014): 8.

results in weakened preachers who have lost their confidence in the message they are called to proclaim. Inevitably, Lawson maintains, weak pulpits result in weak Christians.

Defining the sufficiency of Scripture, Lawson writes, "[By sufficiency,] we mean the ability of God's Word to produce any and all spiritual results intended by God, when it is accompanied by the supreme power of the Holy Spirit."[2] For Lawson, the doctrine of the sufficiency of Scripture affirms that everything *necessary* for the spiritual well-being of individuals, in salvation and sanctification as well as direction for gospel ministry, is found in God's Word.

Lawson also maintains that Scripture itself affirms its own sufficiency. He points to Hebrews 4:12 as evidence: "For the word of God is living and powerful, and sharper than any two-edged sword, piercing even to the division of soul and spirit, and of joints and marrow, and is a discerner of the thoughts and intents of the heart." The Bible claims to be "living," meaning it is full of divine life, supernatural life, the life of God Himself. Lawson comments, "Every other book is a dead book, devoid of life. But not the Bible. It alone is alive, always relevant, never stagnant."[3] Lawson agrees with the German Reformer Martin Luther that "the Bible is alive, it speaks to me; it has feet, it runs after me; it has hands, it lays hold on me."[4]

According to Hebrews 4:12, Scripture also affirms itself to be "active." Interestingly, this is the same Greek word from which we derive the English word "energy." Lawson observes, "This is to say, when Scripture is preached, it is always *energetic*, always *working*, always *executing* God's sovereign purposes."[5] God affirmed through the prophet Isaiah,

> So shall My word be that goes forth from My mouth;
> It shall not return to Me void,
> But it shall accomplish what I please,
> And it shall prosper in the thing for which I sent it. (Isa. 55:11)

God has promised that when His Word is proclaimed, it will accomplish the eternal purpose for which it was intended by His own perfect will. In short, Scripture never fails to succeed in the work for which it is intended.

---

2. Lawson, "Sufficiency of Scripture," 7.

3. Lawson, "Sufficiency of Scripture," 8.

4. As quoted in *More Gathered Gold*, comp. John Blanchard (Durham, England: Evangelical Press, 1984), 26.

5. Lawson, "Sufficiency of Scripture," 8.

Lawson firmly believes that the Bible is an infallible guide to those who follow it and that it addresses all the essential areas of life. He says, "The Scripture has all ability to lead our lives in the direction they should take. The Word is more than adequate to shine light into man's chaos and confusion, replacing ignorance and lack of understanding with lucid direction, eternal perspective, and divine insight."[6] In the course of ministry, this firmly held doctrine and belief in the sufficiency of Scripture has enabled Lawson to stand behind the pulpit with firm confidence and conviction that what he is preaching is absolute truth and the word of God.

This belief has likewise given him the freedom to proclaim boldly all parts of Scripture. Lawson has never shied away from the misunderstood or controversial passages of Scripture. Even when he was told in one church not to preach certain texts in the book of Romans because of their controversial nature, he ardently refused, believing that it is God's Word that transforms the heart rather than ingenuity of speech or eloquent words. Lawson stands in a long line of other preachers through the centuries who have refused to waver on the sufficiency, infallibility, and inerrancy of Scripture.

Theologically Passionate

Theological conviction is the blazing furnace behind Lawson's passionate preaching. He not only stands in the pulpit firmly anchored in the truth of God's Word but also upon the theological positions proclaimed by that Word. Lawson is passionate about the doctrine of God and everything that it includes.

Lawson's system of theology begins with the glory of God. The unrivaled preeminence of God stands as the focal point of his theological universe. Scripture commands, according to Lawson, that God is to be the chief object of praise. In answering the question of what God's glory is, he comments, "The Bible speaks of God's glory in two primary ways. First, there is the *intrinsic* glory of God, which is the sum total of all His divine perfections and attributes.... Second, the Bible also speaks of the *ascribed* glory of God, or the glory that is given to Him."[7] He continues, "This, then, is the centerpiece of God's saving purpose in the universe—the revelation and magnification

6. Lawson, "Sufficiency of Scripture," 10.
7. Steven J. Lawson, *Foundations of Grace* (Lake Mary, Fla.: Reformation Trust, 2006), 31–32.

of His own glory."[8] This is to be the passionate heartbeat of all Christians, especially those who stand to preach: the promotion of the glory of God.

This intrinsic and resplendent glory is most magnificently displayed, as Lawson states, in the doctrines of grace. He writes, "Here, all three members of the Godhead—God the Father, God the Son, and God the Holy Spirit— work together as *one* Savior, indivisibly united in rescuing radically corrupt sinners."[9] He continues:

> Before time began, the Bible teaches, God the Father chose a people for Himself to be worshipers of His glory by becoming the objects of His grace. As an expression of His infinite love for His Son, the Father gave His elect to Christ as a love gift, a people who would praise Him forever and ever. The Father commissioned His Son to come into this world in order to redeem these chosen ones through His sacrificial death. The Father, along with the Son, also sent the Spirit into this world to apply the saving work of the Son to this same group of elect sinners. This vast number of redeemed saints—those *elected* by God, *purchased* by Christ, and *called* by the Spirit—will never fall from grace. They all shall be transported to heaven and glorified forever.[10]

In essence, these marvelous truths are grounded in five main headings that showcase the glory of God in man's salvation. According to Lawson, each of these truths is deeply rooted and solidly grounded in the rich soil of God's Word. He says, "When the Bible is rightly exegeted, carefully expounded, and properly explained, it clearly teaches these truths, which have been identified as total depravity, unconditional election, limited atonement, irresistible grace, and the perseverance of the saints."[11] In short, these doctrinal convictions form the theological position of Calvinism, which, Lawson says, "is a God-centered, Christ-exalting way of viewing salvation."[12] Calvinism identifies God as the only Savior and therefore the only object of rightful praise. He writes, "God alone supplies all that is necessary, both the grace *and* the faith."[13] Anything short of this robs God of glory, and we are

---

8. Lawson, *Foundations of Grace*, 32.
9. Lawson, *Foundations of Grace*, 32.
10. Lawson, *Foundations of Grace*, 33.
11. Lawson, *Foundations of Grace*, 33.
12. Lawson, *Foundations of Grace*, 33.
13. Lawson, *Foundations of Grace*, 33.

reminded, "I am the LORD, that is My name; and My glory I will not give to another" (Isa. 42:8).

Lawson did not always hold to the doctrines of grace. But as he grew in his knowledge and study of God's Word and came under the teaching, preaching, and guidance of men such as R. C. Sproul, James Montgomery Boice, and John MacArthur, he became convinced this was the clear teaching of Scripture. He writes, "The doctrines of grace are a cohesive system of theology in which the sovereignty of God is clearly displayed in the salvation of elect sinners."[14] This cohesive system has shaped and influenced every sermon Lawson has preached, and his pursuit of the glory of God has shaped every act of ministry he has performed. It is from these doctrines, handed down from Jesus, Paul, Augustine, John Calvin, John Owen, Jonathan Edwards, Charles Spurgeon, Martyn Lloyd-Jones, and many others, that Lawson derives the passion of his heart for the preaching of the Word of God—that sinners may be drawn to Him and that He may be glorified.

Expositionally Called

From the very beginning, when Lawson first began to sense the call of God upon his life to enter ministry, he was convinced that he was being called to be a preacher. David Martyn Lloyd-Jones, the great expositor of Westminster Chapel in London, during a lecture series given on preaching at Westminster Theological Seminary, stated, "The most urgent need in the Christian Church today is true preaching; and as it is the greatest and most urgent need in the Church, it is the greatest need of the world also."[15] Lawson echoes the words of this English pulpiteer. He says, "A return to preaching—*true* preaching, *biblical* preaching, *expository* preaching—is the greatest need of this critical hour. If a reformation is to come to the church, it must be preceded by a reformation of the pulpit. As the pulpit goes, so goes the church."[16]

What is expository preaching? Lawson's definition is succinct and straightforward: "It is the man of God opening the Word of God and expounding its truths so that the voice of God may be heard, the glory of God seen, and the will of God obeyed."[17] More specifically, Lawson looks to

---

14. Lawson, *Foundations of Grace*, 30.

15. Martyn Lloyd-Jones, *Preaching and Preachers* (Grand Rapids: Zondervan, 1971), 9.

16. Steven J. Lawson, *Famine in the Land: A Passionate Call for Expository Preaching* (Chicago: Moody Publishers, 2003), 17.

17. Lawson, *Famine in the Land*, 18.

the Genevan Reformer John Calvin for a more detailed definition. Calvin stated that preaching involves the explication of Scripture, the unfolding of its natural and true meaning, while making application to the life and experience of the congregation.[18] Calvin further stated, "Preaching is the public exposition of Scripture by the man sent from God, in which God Himself is present in judgment and in grace."[19] Lawson's view is in accord with Calvin's, which strikes at the heart of what expository preaching truly is.

Biblical preaching, according to Lawson, must come from the life of one who is fervent for the glory of God, zealous for the Word of God, and aflame for the souls of men, women, and youth. He points to the pattern that the apostle Paul gave to Timothy for him to follow in his own pulpit (1 Tim. 4:13). Timothy's ministry was to consist of three parts—the public reading of Scripture, exhortation, and teaching. Lawson affirms, "These three components are the strong and sturdy pillars on which all biblical preaching should rest."[20]

First, the preacher is to read the Word. This refers to the public reading of Scripture in the corporate gathering of the church's worship, a practice dating back to the time of the prophet Ezra (Neh. 8:1–8). Lawson recognizes the centrality of Scripture reading in the worship of the early church. For instance, underscoring the central importance of the Scriptures in the life of the church, John Calvin noted that Paul "places reading before doctrine and exhortation; for, undoubtedly, the Scripture is the fountain of all wisdom, from which pastors must draw all that they place before their flock."[21] Lawson believes the preacher is to be the worship leader during the gathering of the church and that he should therefore follow Paul's instruction to read the Scriptures publicly.

Second, Paul instructed Timothy to accompany reading with "exhortation." Lawson points out that the word "exhortation" (*paraklesis*) means "to come alongside" with the purpose of helping someone who is weak or wayward.[22] This refers to the element of preaching that applies the Word of God to the people's lives. The preacher must not only read the Word of God

---

18. John H. Leigh, "Calvin's Doctrine of the Proclamation of the Word and Its Significance for Today in the Light of Recent Research," *Review and Expositor* 86 (1989): 32, 34.

19. As quoted in *Gathered Gold*, comp. John Blanchard (Grand Rapids: Zondervan, 1955), 33.

20. Lawson, *Famine in the Land*, 112.

21. *Calvin's Commentaries* (repr., Grand Rapids: Baker, 1984), 11:115.

22. Lawson, *Famine in the Land*, 113.

to the people but must also exhort them to obey it. This is where the living element of the Word of God initiates life within the hearts of the hearers. This exhortation may take many forms—instruction, warning, rebuke, edification, counsel, comfort, but, according to John MacArthur, "always involves a binding of the conscience."[23] Thus, Lawson believes that the ultimate goal of Bible exposition is changed lives. He says, "Preaching must do more than simply inform the mind; it must grip the heart and challenge the will. The entire person—mind, emotion, and will—must be impacted. Exposition is not merely for the transmitting of information; it is for the effecting of transformation."[24] So not only is the preacher to publicly read the Scripture but he is also to properly apply its truths to listeners' lives.

Third, preaching must include "teaching" or, more literally, "the teaching" (*didaskalia*), which refers to the explanation of the biblical text. This, according to Lawson, is the careful unfolding of the meaning of the passage. In short, the text must be explained. Drawing a distinction between "exhortation" and "teaching," he says, "While 'exhortation' is more application-oriented, 'teaching' is more doctrine-oriented."[25] To teach the Scriptures is to get to the heart of the passage and the veil, as it were, that hides the face of God. This properly captures what Martyn Lloyd-Jones believed being biblical meant: "My idea of being biblical is that you bring out the real message, the treasure of the Scriptures."[26] This is why serious preparation is required, for the preacher integrates each biblical text into the larger system of theology and shows how each passage, each word, each phrase fits perfectly into the whole counsel of God. Lawson writes, "The expositor is to demonstrate how all biblical truth fits together."[27] He believes this involves disciplined, rigorous study in God's Word. He notes, "All this requires the pastor's personal study in the original languages, historical background, authorial intent, cross-references, cultural background, geography, grammar, literary structure, and systematic theology."[28] Such diligent study is entirely necessary if the true meaning of the biblical text is to be conveyed.

According to Lawson, these three elements—the reading, exhortation, and teaching—are essential for true biblical preaching. These three elements

---

23. John MacArthur Jr., *1 Timothy* (Chicago: Moody Publishers, 1995), 176.
24. Lawson, *Famine in the Land*, 114.
25. Lawson, *Famine in the Land*, 115.
26. D. M. Lloyd-Jones, *Knowing the Times* (Edinburgh: Banner of Truth, 2013), 268.
27. Lawson, *Famine in the Land*, 115.
28. Lawson, *Famine in the Land*, 116.

are all present in Lawson's preaching, and his commitment to these principles has shaped his pulpit ministry to be one of strong, biblical exposition impacting countless lives with transforming truth.

Holding Forth the Torch of Truth

In every generation, God providentially gifts His church with men who are committed to His Word, passionate about His glory, and dedicated to His calling. One such man for our current generation is Steven J. Lawson. His life has been dedicated to biblical exposition and the proclamation of the truth. His desire is to train a new army of gospel heralds who will be unleashed upon a sin-soaked world. His heart is to call the modern evangelical church back to the biblical command to "preach the word" (2 Tim. 4:2).

As Lawson has often stated, "Evangelical churches need to recapture the power of biblical preaching—preaching that is courageous, compelling, confrontative, and compassionate."[29] When Charles H. Spurgeon observed the decline of dynamic preaching in his own day, he pleaded for the Lord to raise up a new generation of biblical preachers.

> We want again Luthers, Calvins, Bunyans, Whitefields, men fit to mark eras, whose names breathe terror in our foemen's ears. We have dire need of such. Whence will they come to us? They are the gifts of Jesus Christ to the Church, and will come in due time. He has power to give us back again a golden age of preachers, and when the good old truth is once more preached by men whose lips are touched as with a live coal from off the altar, this shall be the instrument in the hand of the Spirit for bringing about a great and thorough revival of religion in the land.
>
> I do not look for any other means of converting men beyond the simple preaching of the gospel and the opening of men's ears to hear it. The moment the Church of God shall despise the pulpit, God will despise her. It has been through the ministry that the Lord has always been pleased to revive and bless His Churches.[30]

Lawson comments, "May God raise up such proclaimers of His divine truth who will preach with growing confidence in the power of His Word to perform its sacred work. May Christ give to His church again an army of

---

29. Lawson, *Famine in the Land*, 75.
30. Charles Haddon Spurgeon, *The Early Years* (London: Banner of Truth, 1962), 1:v.

biblical expositors who will proclaim the Scriptures boldly in the power of the Holy Spirit."[31]

As Steven Lawson stood in the pulpit of Christ Fellowship Baptist Church for his final sermon in the summer of 2014, he preached the message he has been preaching for the past thirty years: "Stand firm in the Lord" (Phil. 4:1 NASB). This has been his call to three separate congregations and countless Christians who have heard him preach at conferences around the world. With bold passion, Lawson answers the call he extends to others, standing firm in the faith and holding forth the torch of truth.

31. Lawson, *Famine in the Land*, 75–76.

PART 1

The Mandate of Preaching

CHAPTER 2

A Biblical Priority:
Preach the Word

John MacArthur

More than thirty-five years ago I wrote a book (one of my earliest) titled *The Ultimate Priority*. It is a book about worship, and it makes this simple argument: If, as the Westminster Catechism says, "man's chief end is to glorify God, and to enjoy Him forever," then worship ought to be our highest priority in all of life. That is simply an echo of what Scripture says in 1 Corinthians 10:31: "Whether you eat or drink, or whatever you do, do all to the glory of God." Colossians 3:17 says the same thing in slightly different words: "Whatever you do in word or deed, do all in the name of the Lord Jesus, giving thanks to God the Father through Him." The whole life of the Christian should be a long crescendo of worship.

People today often use the word "worship" to signify the music portion of a church service. The "worship leader" is the person who leads the musicians and congregation in singing. People sometimes even speak of worship as something distinct from the preaching of God's Word. A pastor once told me his church was altering its order of worship to allocate less time for preaching and more time for "worship." My reply was that the preaching of the Word ought to be the heart of corporate worship.

That is the clear pattern we observe in the New Testament. From Pentecost on, the ministry of God's Word is at the heart of what the Holy Spirit was doing in the church. Acts 2:42 outlines the whole agenda of the early church: "They continued steadfastly in the apostles' doctrine and fellowship, in the breaking of bread, and in prayers." One of the earliest accounts of a corporate gathering occurs in Acts 4: "The place where they were assembled together was shaken; and they were all filled with the Holy Spirit, and *they spoke the word of God with boldness*" (v. 31, emphasis added). When other urgent activities threatened to overwhelm church leaders, the apostles said, "We will give ourselves continually to prayer and to the ministry of the word" (Acts 6:4).

Throughout the book of Acts, whenever church leaders are mentioned, they are engaged in the preaching of the Word; and when people are converted, the Word of God is cited as the instrumental cause (8:14, 25; 10:44; 11:1, 19; 13:5, 7, 44–48; 14:3, 25; 15:7, 35–36; 16:32). Clearly the preaching of God's Word was the central activity of the early church.

In fact, when Luke records the growth of the church, he measures it by reporting on the increase in preaching: "The word of God spread" (Acts 6:7). "The word of God grew and multiplied" (Acts 12:24). "The word of the Lord was being spread throughout all the region" (Acts 13:49). "So the word of the Lord grew mightily and prevailed" (Acts 19:20). When persecution forced believers into exile, Scripture says, "Therefore those who were scattered went everywhere preaching the word" (Acts 8:4).

So the heart of corporate worship in the early church was the proclamation of God's Word. That means if worship is the ultimate priority for us as Christians, then worship is what must dominate our corporate gatherings. And preaching is the first and most important aspect of our worship. That is why all the apostle's instructions to young pastors is summed up at the pinnacle of his final epistle to Timothy: "Preach the word! Be ready in season and out of season. Convince, rebuke, exhort, with all longsuffering and teaching" (2 Tim. 4:2).

Why has preaching been in decline for the past half century or so? Let's face it: The whole idea of preaching cuts against the grain of our postmodern, egalitarian society. Modern people are bred and trained to be suspicious of authority of all types. And in an increasingly secular culture, the strongest hostility is reserved for the man who claims to speak by God's authority. So the preacher who dares to preach God's Word with any degree of boldness instantly finds himself at cross-purposes with the spirit of the age.

Many young preachers are therefore timid about the whole notion of preaching. I knew of one pastoral intern who was responsible to fill the pulpit on Sunday evenings twice a month. Invariably he would opt to do something besides preaching. He would lead the congregation in a time of prayer, show a video, conduct a panel discussion, have someone give a testimony, sponsor a musical program, or invite a guest speaker to fill the time. It seemed he would do anything to avoid having to preach. Asked why he never preached, he said, "Oh, I don't know. I don't think people need me to preach at them. I'd rather give them something they'll enjoy. To me the very word 'preaching' sounds arrogant and egotistical." At the peak of the emerging church fad in 2004, one of the movement's most influential leaders famously said,

"Preaching is broken." He said his church had eliminated church pews and preaching in favor of couches and conversation. "Why do I get to speak for thirty minutes and you don't?" he asked. He went on to describe preaching as "a violent act…violence toward the will of the people who have to sit there and take it."[1]

D. Martyn Lloyd-Jones noticed a trend in this direction more than twenty years ago. In a famous series of lectures later published in his book *Preaching and Preachers*, he observed that modern society was becoming uncomfortable with the whole idea of preaching:

> A new idea has crept in with regard to preaching, and it has taken various forms. A most significant one was that people began to talk about the "address" in the service instead of the sermon. That in itself was indicative of a subtle change. An "address." No longer the sermon, but an "address" or perhaps even a lecture…. There was a man in the U.S.A. who published a series of books under the significant title of *Quiet Talks. Quiet Talks on Prayer*; *Quiet Talks on Power*, etc. In other words the very title announces that the man is not going to preach. Preaching, of course, is something carnal lacking in spirituality, what is needed is a chat, a fireside chat, quiet talks, and so on![2]

The situation today is much worse than Lloyd-Jones could ever have imagined. The modern obsession with pragmatic and postmodern ministry styles has stoked the fear of preaching into a pervasive phobia. Seminaries now train men to be storytellers, entertainers, and motivational speakers—and discourage them from dealing with profound or difficult theological concepts from the pulpit. One best-selling resource on ministry to the baby-boom generation gives pastors this advice: "Limit your preaching to roughly 20 minutes…. Keep your messages light and informal, liberally sprinkling them with humor and personal anecdotes."[3] Suddenly "too much Scripture" is deemed a greater homiletical faux pas than a whole sermon with no reference to Scripture whatsoever! In some circles it is perfectly acceptable to give a motivational lecture or comedy routine practically devoid of any biblical content, but a

---

1. Tom Allen, "Postmoderns Value Authenticity, Not Authority," *The Baptist Standard*, July 8, 2004.

2. D. Martyn Lloyd-Jones, *Preaching and Preachers* (Grand Rapids: Zondervan, 1971), 15–16.

3. Doug Murren, *The Baby Boomerang* (Ventura, Calif.: Regal, 1990), 103.

verse-by-verse exposition of Scripture would automatically be deemed too weighty and (this is the unpardonable sin) insufficiently "relevant."

Meanwhile, real preachers, men willing to stand in the pulpit, open the Word of God, and proclaim it with authority and conviction, are in seriously short supply. It seems the whole church is seized with a fear of preaching.

The apostle Paul was addressing that fear in his second epistle to Timothy. Timothy was a close disciple and choice student of the apostle Paul. But in a pastorate of his own, cut off from his mentor, young Timothy struggled with fear. He was tempted to tone down his message. He was hindered by his own fear of preaching. So the apostle Paul wrote to urge him to stand up boldly for the faith, even if that meant he would suffer as Paul himself was suffering: "Do not be ashamed of the testimony of our Lord, nor of me His prisoner, but share with me in the sufferings for the gospel" (2 Tim. 1:8).

Paul foresaw a time when it would become even harder to preach boldly, when congregations would not tolerate sound doctrine or fearless preaching, when people would deliberately turn away from the truth (2 Tim. 4:3–4). If Timothy was struggling under mild opposition, what would he do when he faced real persecution? What would he do when called upon to minister to people with no appetite for the Word and no tolerance for bold preaching? Would he accommodate his hearers' preferences or be faithful to his calling? He could not do both. Paul's advice left no room for compromise: "Preach the word! Be ready in season and out of season. Convince, rebuke, exhort, with all longsuffering and teaching" (2 Tim. 4:2).

Clearly, "seeker sensitivity" was the furthest thing from Paul's mind. He urged Timothy to preach the Word boldly, even if that is not what the crowds are clamoring for. People's ears may be itching for anything but sound doctrine, but the faithful pastor will defy the spirit of the age, confront his own fear, and boldly preach the truth anyway. Paul longed to see that kind of boldness in his young disciple.

Several factors could have contributed to Timothy's fear. It might have been sparked by a desire for accolades from his congregation—or fear that people might leave if they did not like him. It might have been a reaction to criticism he had received. People may have deliberately intimidated him because of his own youthful age (1 Tim. 4:12). Nonetheless, Paul encouraged Timothy to persevere faithfully in the task, despite people's response. Far from reassuring Timothy about how beloved he would be, Paul warned him that he would suffer hardship.

The very heart of Paul's advice to Timothy in this epistle is found at the beginning of 2 Timothy 4. This brief passage sums up the whole gist of 2 Timothy:

> I charge you therefore before God and the Lord Jesus Christ, who will judge the living and the dead at His appearing and His kingdom: Preach the word! Be ready in season and out of season. Convince, rebuke, exhort, with all longsuffering and teaching. For the time will come when they will not endure sound doctrine, but according to their own desires, because they have itching ears, they will heap up for themselves teachers; and they will turn their ears away from the truth, and be turned aside to fables. But you be watchful in all things, endure afflictions, do the work of an evangelist, fulfill your ministry. (vv. 1–5)

In the space of those five verses, the apostle Paul gives Timothy an effective antidote for the fear of preaching in nine simple imperatives.

Remember to Whom You Are Accountable

When Paul wrote this epistle to Timothy, the apostle was near the end of his life. (This was the last inspired epistle he wrote. Shortly afterward, he would be executed for his faith.) And these words begin the closing section of the epistle: "I charge you therefore before God and the Lord Jesus Christ, who will judge the living and the dead at His appearing and His kingdom" (v. 1).

Paul was looking forward to a time not far in the future when he would stand before God to give an account, and his own anticipation of judgment no doubt filled his heart and mind. So he reminded Timothy that the young pastor would also one day be called to give an account before God. He was urging Timothy to live and work in light of impending judgment. In other words, Timothy needed to fear God more than he feared the opinions of people.

"We shall all stand before the judgment seat of Christ.... So then each of us shall give account of himself to God" (Rom. 14:10, 12). The preacher who focuses on his accountability to God is less likely to be stymied by the fear of human opinion.

Preach the Word

These three simple words sum up all the apostle's advice to Timothy, spanning two epistles: "Preach the word!" (v. 2). No fear is legitimate if it dissuades the preacher from that task. No philosophy of pastoral ministry is sound if it has anything else as its main focus.

Preaching the Word is by no means always easy. The faithful preacher will not always get accolades. In fact, those who are faithful are guaranteed persecution (2 Tim. 3:12). It is easy to become fearful. The pulpit is no place for a timid man.

Furthermore, the message we are called to proclaim is an offense and a stumbling block to many (1 Cor. 1:23; Gal. 5:11), and mere foolishness to others (1 Cor. 1:23). Christ Himself is a stone of stumbling and a rock of offense (Rom. 9:33; 1 Peter 2:8). The faithful preacher will inevitably meet with hostility and rejection. It is not a task for the faint of heart.

Timothy evidently was prone to fear. Paul reminded him that "God has not given us a spirit of fear, but of power and of love and of a sound mind"—and urged him not to be "ashamed of the testimony of our Lord, nor of me His prisoner" (2 Tim. 1:7–8). It seems Timothy was a naturally timid soul. His personality certainly contrasts starkly with that of the bold and courageous apostle who mentored him.

Timothy had seen his mentor suffer for the faith. In fact, he had witnessed Paul's hardships up close, and now he was no doubt hearing that things were going even worse for Paul. Even being associated with Paul probably put Timothy in great danger. Preaching the gospel publicly in Ephesus certainly would have exposed him to the wrath of civil officials and Jews who were hostile to Christ.

So Timothy daily faced the real prospect that he might be called upon to suffer or die for the gospel's sake. No wonder he was afraid to preach. When Paul urged him to proclaim God's Word boldly, he was urging him to go against every natural human inclination and inhibition.

Paul also emphasized that Timothy was to preach only one message: the Word. Just before this charge, Paul had reminded Timothy of the vital authority and power of God's Word. "*All Scripture* is given by inspiration of God, and is profitable for doctrine, for reproof, for correction, for instruction in righteousness" (2 Tim. 3:16, emphasis added). And back in chapter 1 the apostle wrote, "Hold fast the pattern of sound words which you have heard from me" (v. 13). He urged Timothy to "keep by the Holy Spirit who dwells in us" the "good thing" that was committed to him (v. 14; cf. 1 Tim. 6:20). He implored the young pastor to devote himself to studying the Word and handling it accurately (2 Tim. 2:15). And here he commands him to preach the Word boldly despite his natural fears and apprehensions. Virtually all the counsel Paul has given Timothy therefore comes to a focus in this command to preach the Word. Faithfully preaching the Word was the heart of his calling as a pastor.

The apostle Paul assessed his own duty as a minister in Colossians 1:25, explaining that for the sake of the church "I became a minister according to the stewardship from God which was given to me for you, *to fulfill the word of God*" (emphasis added). Elsewhere he wrote, "I, brethren, when I came to you, did not come with excellence of speech or of wisdom declaring to you the testimony of God. For I determined not to know anything among you except Jesus Christ and Him crucified" (1 Cor. 2:1–2). Thus he sums up his supreme priority in the task of preaching, both as a pastor and as an evangelist.

Pastors must not allow fear, public opinion, or pragmatic methodology to dissuade them from boldly preaching the Word. No aspect of church ministry is more vital than this. And the church that substitutes entertainment, moral lectures, motivational talks, or anything else in the place of preaching the Word has abdicated its high calling.

Be Faithful In and Out of Season

Preaching is the nonnegotiable heart of the church's ministry. This fact does not change because public opinion changes. Some people today argue that the church could draw more "unchurched" people by featuring drama and music instead of preaching. But Paul's instructions to Timothy were clear. He was to preach the Word whether preaching was popular or not—"in season and out of season" (2 Tim. 4:2).

There is no question that we are living in an era when preaching the Word is "out of season." But the faithful pastor will preach the Word boldly, clearly, and faithfully anyway because that is precisely what this passage commands.

The King James Version says, "Be instant in season, out of season." This is an archaic use of the word "instant." During that period "instant" meant readiness, preparedness, availability, and eagerness. The Greek word translated "instant" is a military term that literally means "to stand beside." It was used of a guard who was always at his post, on the watch, prepared. Timothy was supposed to be ready, zealous to preach, eager to preach—even when society as a whole was not particularly ready to hear. He was not to give in to the fear of preaching.

Reprove, Rebuke, and Exhort

The apostle Paul further specified what kind of preaching Timothy was to do. All good preaching includes these elements: reproof, rebuke, and exhortation. Note that two of these have negative connotations, involving correction of error or wrong behavior. Exhortation, by contrast, is positive. All preaching should have this balance. The preacher who tries to be always positive is not fulfilling his commission. Exposing and correcting error is as integral to the preacher's task as proclaiming the truth (see Titus 1:9).

Moreover, the preacher who proclaims the whole counsel of God will maintain a proper balance because reproving, rebuking, and exhorting are precisely what Scripture itself does: "All Scripture is given by inspiration of God, and is profitable for doctrine, for reproof, for correction, for instruction in righteousness" (2 Tim. 3:16). Notice the same balance of correction (the negative) and instruction (the positive).

While the faithful preacher will not shy away from rebuke and correction, his ultimate aim is always edification and encouragement. And he stays at the task "with all longsuffering and teaching" (2 Tim. 4:2). Paul himself had been Timothy's example. "As you know how we exhorted, and comforted, and charged every one of you, as a father does his own children, that you would walk worthy of God who calls you into His own kingdom and glory" (1 Thess. 2:11–12).

Don't Compromise in Difficult Times

If Timothy was already struggling with the fear of preaching, he was facing even more difficult times in the days to come: "For the time will come when they will not endure sound doctrine, but according to their own desires, because they have itching ears, they will heap up for themselves teachers; and they will turn their ears away from the truth, and be turned aside to fables" (2 Tim. 4:3–4). This sort of warning was a persistent theme in Paul's correspondence with Timothy. Notice 1 Timothy 4:1: "Now the Spirit expressly says that in latter times some will depart from the faith, giving heed to deceiving spirits and doctrines of demons"; and 2 Timothy 3:1–5:

> But know this, that in the last days perilous times will come: For men will be lovers of themselves, lovers of money, boasters, proud, blasphemers, disobedient to parents, unthankful, unholy, unloving, unforgiving, slanderers, without self-control, brutal, despisers of good, traitors, headstrong, haughty, lovers of pleasure rather than lovers of

God, having a form of godliness but denying its power. And from such people turn away!

There is a kind of progression in those warnings. First, Paul said a time was coming when people would depart from the faith. Then he warned Timothy that dangerous times were coming for the church. Here he suggests that a time would come when even people in the church would not endure sound doctrine but would desire instead to have their ears tickled.

In such times, fearless preaching is only more vital. When intolerance of the truth is heightened, the need for bold preachers is also heightened. But when preachers tone down their message to accommodate the spirit of the age, they play into the enemy's scheme.

Ear-tickling preaching is the opposite of what Paul expected from Timothy. When popular opinion demands preachers who are palatable to the tastes of the audience (2 Tim. 4:3), fearful preachers are always tempted to capitulate to the demand. Paul hoped to see better from his young disciple.

What the apostle Paul warned Timothy about is coming to pass virtually before our eyes: "People will not endure sound teaching, but having itching ears they will accumulate for themselves teachers to suit their own passions." There is no shortage of teachers today. But the overwhelming mass of them cater to the tastes of their audience—precisely what Paul warned against. They want to minister to people's "felt needs." They are obsessed with being "relevant." They think too much doctrine or too much Scripture is a turn-off to the "unchurched" people they want to reach. They allow opinion polls to determine the content of their message. Their greatest fear is offending their hearers. This style of ministry is often labeled "seeker sensitive" or "user friendly," but Scripture calls it ear tickling.

Whenever fear silences bold preaching, ear-tickling teachers will always rush in to fill the void. Marvin R. Vincent, a commentator from another generation, saw this same trend in his era: "In periods of unsettled faith, skepticism, and mere curious speculation in matters of religion, teachers of all kinds swarm like the flies in Egypt. The demand creates the supply. The hearers invite and shape their own preachers. If the people desire a calf to worship, a ministerial calf-maker is readily found."[4]

---

4. Marvin R. Vincent, *Word Studies in the New Testament* (New York: Scribner's, 1900), 4:321.

Feeding an appetite for ear-tickling teachers leads inevitably to spiritual catastrophe. People who, "according to their own desires, because they have itching ears,... will heap up for themselves teachers" ultimately "will turn their ears away from the truth, and be turned aside to fables" (2 Tim. 4:3–4). Their own deliberate refusal to hear the truth predictably leads them into error.

This whole passage perfectly chronicles the course of the evangelical movement in our generation. What the apostle Paul predicted has unfolded before our eyes. Evangelicals have lost their tolerance for bold, confrontational, biblical preaching. People have demanded to be entertained. Pastors, fearful of losing their people's approval, have acquiesced to public opinion. And now the church, on several fronts, is flirting with serious doctrinal error, unable to distinguish truth from falsehood. Having turned aside from the truth, it is susceptible to myths.

We see this tendency in numerous trends. Evangelicals have largely forgotten or relinquished the distinctive principles of *sola fide* and *sola Scriptura*. Some even seem critical of the Protestant Reformation, acting as if all Protestant–Roman Catholic differences grew out of an unnecessarily divisive spirit. Millions of charismatics are engaged in a mad pursuit of extrabiblical revelation, prophecies, dreams, and mystical experience. Many evangelicals are openly skeptical about whether hell really involves everlasting punishment. Christians are willing to reinterpret virtually all the difficult teachings of Scripture to try to make Christianity politically correct. All these trends are fruits of pulpits paralyzed by fear.

When a preacher becomes fearful of what people think, the temptation is powerful to tone down the message, trim the difficult parts, and preach a message people will like. But the faithful, fearless preacher will not—and must not—succumb to such pressures.

Be Sober-Minded

The antidote to carnal fear is a godly sobriety. Paul tells Timothy, "Be watchful [or, in some translations, sober-minded] in all things" (2 Tim. 4:5). Obviously Paul was not warning Timothy against drunkenness. (In his first epistle, Paul had to urge Timothy to stop drinking water exclusively because Timothy's health was suffering, possibly from amoeba in the unpurified water. So Timothy was clearly a man not given to much wine, and the sobriety Paul enjoins here has nothing to do with Timothy's drinking habits.) Nor was Paul suggesting that Timothy should adopt a morose, dreary, joyless demeanor. Paul was calling him to alertness, stability, and self-control—a steadiness of character that would counteract Timothy's susceptibility to fear.

Paul was urging Timothy to mature into manhood, to be steady and serious-minded, to bring his passions—and especially his fears—under complete control. This kind of sobriety is the polar opposite of the flaky, whimsical, superficial, celebrity-type televangelists who color the public perception of preachers today. The faithful preacher should be well rooted and grounded, steadfast, stable—rock solid. What Paul was calling for is the antithesis of fear.

Endure Suffering

As we have noted, a yearning for earthly applause underlies much of the fear that has paralyzed the modern pulpit. Too many preachers have an unhealthy fixation with earthly standards of success. The temptation is strong for some men in the ministry to indulge people's preferences simply to avoid the hardship that usually follows when people are offended at our message.

But hardship is an inevitable by-product of all faithful ministry. "All who desire to live godly in Christ Jesus will suffer persecution" (2 Tim. 3:12). The church I pastor shares a campus with the Master's Seminary. We have trained and sent numerous young men into pastoral ministry. Every now and then, one of these young men tells me he hopes to find a church without significant problems—a ministry where he can preach and serve without opposition. The desire is understandable, but there is no such place for the faithful preacher of the Word. Ministry cannot be both effective and painless. Those who preach the Word faithfully must expect to encounter hardship, and they have to be willing to endure such trials, or they will be seized by fear and unable to minister effectively. Hardship, an inevitable part of every faithful preacher's life, must be embraced along with every other aspect of our calling.

In fact, Timothy himself may have been on the verge of severe hardship when Paul wrote this epistle. In the book of Hebrews we read, "Know that our brother Timothy has been set free, with whom I shall see you if he comes shortly" (Heb. 13:23). Evidently, by the time Hebrews was written, Timothy was being released from imprisonment somewhere. So ultimately he did suffer great hardship because of his faithfulness in the ministry. Perhaps the apostle Paul knew such a trial was coming to Timothy when he penned this epistle.

Whatever the historical circumstances, this is a running theme in 2 Timothy. Paul repeatedly addressed Timothy's fear of hardship: "Share with me in the sufferings for the gospel according to the power of God" (1:8). "Be strong in the grace that is in Christ Jesus" (2:1). "You therefore must endure hardship as a good soldier of Jesus Christ" (2:3). He reminded Timothy of the eternal value of suffering for Christ and for the gospel: "Therefore I endure all things for the sake of the elect, that they also may obtain the salvation which is in Christ Jesus with eternal glory" (2:10). And he testified that God's grace had sustained him through his own sufferings, reminding Timothy of the "persecutions, afflictions, which happened to me at Antioch, at Iconium, at Lystra—what persecutions I endured. And out of them all the Lord delivered me" (3:11). And Paul suffered alone.

> At my first defense no one stood with me, but all forsook me. May it not be charged against them.
> But the Lord stood with me and strengthened me, so that the message might be preached fully through me, and that all the Gentiles might hear. Also I was delivered out of the mouth of the lion. (4:16–17)

Paul had faced incredible hardship for years without letup. But the Lord strengthened him, sustained him, and at times pulled him from the jaws of his tormenters. Thus Paul learned to remain faithful and to lean on the Lord for strength, regardless of his circumstances (see Phil. 4:11–13). Paul did not want his young disciple to be paralyzed by fear of hardship and thus miss the blessing he had enjoyed by learning to trust the Lord in the midst of such trials.

Do the Work of an Evangelist

Timothy's fears may have been causing him to seek a comfort zone where he could avoid outreach to people who were not always sympathetic to his ministry. So Paul adds this command: "Do the work of an evangelist" (2 Tim. 4:5). I don't believe Paul meant that Timothy was supposed to fill the office of an evangelist rather than that of a pastor-teacher (see Eph. 4:11). But Paul was indicating evangelism should be part of the work of a pastor too.

This fit perfectly with the gist of Paul's message to Timothy: he was to declare the truth boldly. He had to shed his fear of preaching. He needed to get outside the comfort zone of his own flock. He needed to take his ministry to the front lines, face his opposition courageously, and preach without fear.

Fulfill Your Ministry

Paul sums up his charge to Timothy with this imperative: "Fulfill your ministry" (2 Tim. 4:5). The Greek word translated "fulfill" is *plerophoreo*—meaning "carry it out fully; perform all of it thoroughly." He employs the same word later in verse 17: "The Lord stood with me and strengthened me, so that the message might be preached [*plerophoreo*] fully through me, and that all the Gentiles might hear." He was urging Timothy to the same steadfast fearlessness. He was imploring him not to cave in to halfheartedness and craven fear, but to carry out his ministry with all his might.

Bear in mind that the starting point and the heart of Paul's charge to Timothy is that phrase in verse 2: "Preach the word." All the imperatives that follow simply explain how Timothy was to preach. Thus this passage defines what faithful biblical preaching is to be like: There is no place for timidity. There is no time for delay. There is no latitude for adjusting the message to suit the spirit of the age. The preacher of the Word must be bold, thorough, unrelenting, persevering in the face of hardship and opposition—and above all, fearless.

Anything less is unworthy of a true minister of Christ.

CHAPTER 3

A Pastoral Preeminence: Feed My Sheep

R. C. Sproul

It is a profound blessing that we, at least in the West, have easy access to the Word of God. Nearly every home in America, believing or not, has at least one copy. Most of us have multiple copies, and many of us are able to carry God's Word with us on our smartphones. Like most blessings, however, this one comes with temptations and challenges.

The Danger of the Familiar

The virtual ubiquity of God's Word has not translated into a biblically literate church. We have run into the opposite aphorism of "absence makes the heart grow fonder," finding that familiarity can breed contempt. We have Bibles, but many of us know precious little of them. Even, however, when our possession of the Bible leads to proper study of the Bible, we often face another temptation. In some ways, we know more than we ought. Our familiarity with the Bible can lessen the impact of its many surprises. We tend, for instance, to telescope the history of the Bible. The four hundred long years of prophetic silence that God's people endured between the end of the ministry of Malachi to the announcement of the coming birth of John the forerunner go by, for us, in seconds as we simply turn the page. We miss out on the angst.

We tend, as well, to telescope the lives of the saints. Because we know what will become of Saul, the persecutor of the church, we miss the terror he was to the church, as well as the astonishing choice God made in calling him to minister to the Gentiles. When Peter at Caesarea Philippi has his moment of triumph, boldly proclaiming Jesus to be the Christ, the Son of the living God, we know already that in a few moments, having just been given the name Petros, "the Rock," that he will be given another name, as Jesus says to him, "Get behind Me, Satan!" (Matt. 16:23). Because we know the whole story, we flatten out the peaks and valleys along the way.

This is perhaps no more evident than when we read the gospel narratives between the crucifixion of Christ and His resurrection. One of the reasons the church marks these days is that we might seek to enter into the horror and sorrow of what came in between. But we all know the good news—He is risen! The disciples, however, did not know this. Indeed, even after Jesus appeared to them, there remained much uncertainty and confusion—which is why, I suspect, Peter went fishing. It was something he knew, a familiar pattern, a calming liturgy.

It turned out, however, to be a rough night. Buffeted by his own shame at denying his Lord three times after his bold affirmation he would never do that, Peter found insult added to injury in failing at fishing. All night, and not a fish to show for it! Imagine the burden of his guilt, the temptation and yet fear to hope, the long, grinding hours of futility. Wait before you rush forward to Peter's triumphant sermon at Pentecost and feel the weight of that moment.

> But when the morning had now come, Jesus stood on the shore; yet the disciples did not know that it was Jesus. Then Jesus said to them, "Children, have you any food?"
>
> They answered Him, "No."
>
> And He said to them, "Cast the net on the right side of the boat, and you will find some." So they cast, and now they were not able to draw it in because of the multitude of fish. (John 21:4–6)

Isn't it likely that while one of Peter's challenges was fixed, his confusion grew? This was not the first time that Jesus, the itinerant rabbi, had taught the veteran fisherman how to do his job. Luke records that event:

> When He had stopped speaking, He said to Simon, "Launch out into the deep and let down your nets for a catch."
>
> But Simon answered and said to Him, "Master, we have toiled all night and caught nothing; nevertheless at Your word I will let down the net." And when they had done this, they caught a great number of fish, and their net was breaking. So they signaled to their partners in the other boat to come and help them. And they came and filled both the boats, so that they began to sink. When Simon Peter saw it, he fell down at Jesus' knees, saying, "Depart from me, for I am a sinful man, O Lord!" (Luke 5:4–8)

The first time Jesus told Peter where to fish, Peter responded with fear. He saw in this power the holiness of Jesus, which in turn revealed his own lack of holiness. He wanted to get away as fast as he could. Jesus, however, there and then called Peter to follow Him.

Much has been made—and rightly so—of the similarities and differences between Judas and Peter. Both men, on the same night, betrayed the man they had sat under and labored beside. Both men were overcome with sorrow over what they had done, Judas to the point of suicide. In John's account of the breakfast by the sea, we see the key difference between the two men— "Therefore that disciple whom Jesus loved said to Peter, 'It is the Lord!' Now when Simon Peter heard that it was the Lord, he put on his outer garment (for he had removed it), and plunged into the sea" (John 21:7).

Peter's response to his sorrow was not to flee from Jesus and take his life but to run or, rather, to swim to Jesus for the sake of his life. While the remaining disciples rowed their boat and their catch to the shore, Peter found that he could not wait. When Jesus had appeared earlier, Peter's betrayal had not been dealt with. He did not know what he would find. But he did know whom he would find.

After eating, Jesus turned His attention to Peter:

So when they had eaten breakfast, Jesus said to Simon Peter, "Simon, son of Jonah, do you love Me more than these?"

He said to Him, "Yes, Lord; You know that I love You."

He said to him, "Feed My lambs." (John 21:15)

Twice more Jesus asked the same question, twice more Peter gave the same answer, and twice more Jesus gave the same admonition:

He said to him again a second time, "Simon, son of Jonah, do you love Me?"

He said to Him, "Yes, Lord; You know that I love You."

He said to him, "Tend My sheep."

He said to him the third time, "Simon, son of Jonah, do you love Me?" Peter was grieved because He said to him the third time, "Do you love Me?"

And he said to Him, "Lord, You know all things; You know that I love You."

Jesus said to him, "Feed My sheep." (vv. 16–17)

Much has been made of this threefold repetition. Some have suggested that this was another use of the Hebrew practice of demonstrating emphasis by repetition. When Jesus spoke, "Verily, verily," or "Truly, truly," He was admonishing His audience to give special attention. And, of course, God's holiness is eternally sung by His angels as Isaiah described in His vision, the angels crying out, "Holy, holy, holy is the LORD of hosts; the whole earth is full of His glory" (Isa. 6:3).

While such may be the case, I suspect the threefold repetition had more to do with Peter's grieving heart over his own threefold betrayal of the Lord. In His grace our Lord gives Peter the opportunity, three times, to affirm his love, having denied the same three times just days before. It is a tender moment, and with the balm of the opportunity for Peter to affirm his love, our Lord's method brought with it the sting of the threefold reminder of the threefold betrayal.

There are, however, two other key elements of this dialogue that are easy to miss—one from Peter, the other from Jesus. Note that Peter's "defense" is not grounded in his own integrity. Peter's credibility is at an all-time low. But his reply isn't simply an increasingly loud insistence of his love. Peter does not bring out evidence, highlighting the sacrifice of his following Jesus during His earthly ministry. He doesn't remind Jesus of the glory of his proclamation at Caesarea Philippi. Instead, his only defense of his love is the knowledge of his Lord. Three times Peter not only affirms his love for Jesus but also affirms that Jesus already knows the answer to the question: "You know, O Lord." It is as if he is turning the question back to Jesus. Confused and disappointed by his betrayal, trying to understand how it could not be proof positive of a lack of love, he pleads with Jesus's knowledge.

Note, however, Jesus's response. Jesus is not a celestial supercomputer, Google in the flesh spitting out an accurate answer: "Yes, Peter, your answer is correct. I have done a fresh survey of your heart, and My diagnosis is that you do indeed love Me." Neither does Jesus list the evidence. Instead, He gives a charge—"Feed My sheep." Three times Jesus asks the question. Three times Peter answers in the affirmative, each time citing Jesus's own knowledge of the answer. And three times Jesus makes the same command—"Feed My sheep."

The Danger in the Unfamiliar
While our familiarity with the Bible comes with peculiar dangers, there are also dangers in the many things we are unfamiliar with. Our image of sheep

is hopelessly romantic. We think of them as sweet-tempered, docile animals. The original audience knew better.

The use of sheep as a metaphor for the people of God is striking. We see the relationship of the shepherd to the sheep throughout the canon of Scripture. Psalm 23 is of particular note here. David, himself a shepherd, draws from his own experience to depict the Lord with those wonderful qualities of the shepherd: "The Lord is my shepherd." The first conclusion David draws is that if the Lord is his shepherd, it follows irresistibly that he should not want. For the Good Shepherd does not leave His lambs destitute, starving, in a state of want. That metaphor carries over to the New Testament. In John 10, Jesus declares that He is the Good Shepherd and distinguishes Himself from the hireling who cares for the sheep only as a means of compensation. When the wolf comes, the hireling runs and abandons the sheep. In contrast, the Good Shepherd lays down His life for His sheep.

Anybody in Palestine who knew how dependent sheep were upon their shepherd would grasp the significance of the metaphor. The absolute dependence of the sheep makes it fitting to liken God and His Messiah to the role of the shepherd. But what is perhaps most startling is that the people of God are compared to sheep. If you know anything about sheep, you understand that is not a complimentary metaphor. I remember playing golf once in Michigan. In the middle of the game, we were trying to go down the fairway, and suddenly a flock of sheep wandered across the fairway. It was a flock without a shepherd. We tried to get rid of them, but it was difficult. We could not anticipate their movements. They moved this way, then that way. They sometimes moved backwards, then sideways. They had no direction. They were wandering aimlessly because there was no one to guide them.

While the metaphor of sheep may not be the most flattering, God uses it to describe His own people. The reason calling people sheep is not a complimentary metaphor is because it communicates a kind of stupidity. With respect to the things of God, His sheep—including you and me—are somewhat dense.

But we should not understand the denseness of God's sheep as meaning that we are incapable of learning. During seminary, in homiletics class, I was told that I should never preach above an eighth-grade level to my parishioners. My professor's reasoning was that even if all the parishioners have a college education, they are still infantile in their understanding when it comes to theology and the things of God. When I heard that, I said, "I refuse to submit to that. I will not be satisfied with an eighth-grade education for the people in our church. If that is where they are, we cannot let them stay there. We have to help them grow beyond infancy. We cannot let them be content with a childish faith." We are to depend on God like a child who implicitly and fully trusts in his good father, but we are not to be immature and childish in our understanding of God's Word. The Bible rebukes us for being satisfied with milk and for being unwilling to go on to the meat of the things of God (Heb. 5:12–15).

All of these things make up part of the background in this discussion and show us what Jesus is getting at with regard to the most important task of His undershepherds, those pastors and elders whom Peter later calls to "shepherd the flock of God" (1 Peter 5:2). Undoubtedly, when Peter wrote this text, he had in mind the imagery of sheep that Jesus had used when He had restored him to ministry.

Feed His Sheep

There is, however, a finer precision to the instruction of Jesus. We know from the life of David that a shepherd is called to take great risks for the sake of his sheep. David interposed himself between the flock under his care and a lion and a bear. Hirelings flee at any sign of trouble. True shepherds stand firm. We know from Jesus's parable of the lost sheep that a good shepherd goes out in search of wandering sheep and rejoices over their return. Jesus could have enjoined Peter in this direction and such would have been fitting.

His specific instruction, however, was that Peter would feed *His* sheep. Note the capital *H* in "His." In calling Peter, the fisherman, to the life of a shepherd, He calls him to the life of an undershepherd. The sheep belong to the Good Shepherd, to Jesus Himself. Peter, however, and by extension all of us who serve as undershepherds, must remember to whom the sheep belong. Pastors are placed in a position of taking care of the lambs who were bought and purchased by Jesus. They belong to Him. There is no greater sacred trust than to be entrusted by God with the care of His people.

Jesus, however, calls Peter not just to care for His sheep but to *feed* His sheep. Sheep need to be protected. They need to be herded. But most of all, they need to be fed. What does it mean to feed the lambs? What does it mean to tend the sheep? Food, certainly, is the primary substance by which our bodies are nurtured. What Christ is saying to Peter is, "I am holding you responsible to nurture my sheep. You are to feed them. You are to give them nourishing food."

Jesus did not say, "Peter, if you love Me, poison My sheep." How could a pastor poison the sheep of Christ? Peter tells us in his second epistle. His central concern was the destruction brought upon the people of God by heretics. Peter was concerned about false prophets destroying God's people. He knew their erroneous teaching was the antithesis of nurturing food. He knew they were poisoning the Lord's flock with their false instruction.

We see this same problem in the Old Testament. The greatest threat to the security of Israel was not the Philistines, the Assyrians, the Babylonians, or the Persians. The greatest threat was always the false prophet within the camp. Every time a true prophet would speak a word from God, there would be a hundred other so-called ministers who came to deny it. Jeremiah knew these false prophets well, and he complained about their false promises of peace, their lying visions, and their dreams that denied the Lord God (Jer. 23:9–27). But what did God say was the answer? "The prophet who has a dream, let him tell a dream; and he who has My word, let him speak My word faithfully" (v. 28). Food that has spoiled poisons people. The only food that will nurture the people of God is the food of the truth of the Word of God. The preacher and teacher of God's Word is responsible to proclaim this Word faithfully, even if false prophets are found on every corner.

When pastors get in the pulpit and assume the role of the shepherd and acquiesce to the mandate to feed the sheep, they must feed them the truth. They need to be scrupulous in the time that they spend preparing their sermons to make sure that their understanding of Scripture is accurate. They must work to interpret rightly the Word of God so that they do not distort, bend, falsify, or, even worse, replace it with the opinions of men. Those who are called to preach or teach God's Word must proclaim the truth, not the alternative, which is spiritual poison.

Jesus told Peter to feed His sheep. He did not say, "If you really love Me, Peter, entertain My sheep." There are too many churches in our day that do everything they can to entertain people. They preach an "easy-believism" that fills churches with people who have made a profession of faith and yet do not possess that faith. No one has ever been saved simply by a profession of faith or by attending a church service. Justification is not simply by profession of faith. You have to have that faith in your heart.

The neglect of the Word of God and the focus on "seeker-sensitive" worship can create dangerous environments. In these environments, pastors may have countless sheep in their care who think they are in a state of grace but who will not receive eternal life on the last day. Jesus will look at these so-called sheep and say, "I never knew you; depart from Me, you who practice lawlessness!" (Matt. 7:23).

The principal task of preaching is to nurture the people of God. However, I would be derelict in my duty if I assumed my church was filled with just the redeemed. Every Sunday I know that there are people in my congregation who are not regenerate. If I love them, I have to feed them with the whole counsel of God. I must do whatever is in my power to make sure that these sheep are not lost. And since only the Holy Spirit can save people, the one task that I can perform for the sake of the salvation of the people under my care is the faithful proclamation of the Word of God.

Jesus did not say to Peter, "If you love Me, give them the self-help they need according to the insights of pop psychology." The only thing under heaven that will nurture the sheep under our care is the Word of God. Our people desperately need this food if they are going to know the Good Shepherd.

The Healthy Food of the Gospel

Dietitians will tell you that the calories you consume should come from healthy, nutritious foods—not from junk food. We can apply this principle to spiritual matters and the food of the Word of God. When Jesus says, "Feed My sheep," He is not saying, "Give them fast food." Pastors must make sure that they are not giving Christ's sheep tasty—but unhealthy—food.

Where does junk food come from? On the one hand, there is food like candy, which was never meant to be healthy. On the other hand, junk food can be food that was once perfectly nutritious food. But, after much alteration, it has lost its nutritional value. For example, you can add many refined sugars and fats to a fruity pastry and then fry it. The fruit thus loses its original nutritional qualities, and the food as a whole is actually unhealthy.

Spiritually speaking, we turn the gospel into junk food when we try to improve upon it. In the last sermon he preached, Martin Luther addressed those who thought the gospel was not enough. These were people who wanted to add "devotion to relics" to their faith. They were searching for alternative sources of power besides the gospel. They thought they could find another source of power by "improving" the gospel—by adding another source of power for healing and transformation. Luther rebuked clergy who supported this return to relics because they were departing from the only true source of power, the gospel of Jesus Christ. They were trying to find power where there was no power, only superstition.

In his sermon Luther also addressed the laypeople, pleading with them not to be fooled by impotent articles that had no real power, that is, the relics. He told them to beware those who would try to improve the gospel. He referred to those who were always seeking improvements on the gospel as "jackanapes"—eloquent scoundrels.

The church of Christ is desperately in need of men who will not be jackanapes in the pulpit. It needs laypeople who will not let their pastors become scoundrels who try to improve on the gospel. How do pastors keep themselves from becoming jackanapes, and how do laypeople keep scoundrels out of the pulpit? By knowing the content of the gospel clearly enough that they can spot counterfeits.

How, though, does a faithful undershepherd stay focused on the message? By believing it himself. In God's good providence, Jesus's command to Peter comes not just in the context of Peter's betrayal but in our Lord's promise at that time: "I have prayed for you, that your faith should not fail; and when you have returned to Me, strengthen your brethren" (Luke 22:32). Peter's betrayal is why he must believe the gospel, which in turn is why he must preach the gospel, for undershepherds shepherd best as they remember that they too are sheep, rescued by the Great Shepherd. Undershepherds feed the sheep because they feed with them on the Great Shepherd, whose flesh is food indeed.

CHAPTER 4

A Historical Pedigree:
Sixteenth-Century Reformed Preaching

Joel R. Beeke

The history of the Christian faith can be approached as an account of how God works through the preaching of His Word. The first four centuries of Christianity saw notable missionary expansion and theological clarification, both linked to faithful and powerful preaching. However, when the Council of Chalcedon (451) put the finishing touches on the formulation of the doctrine of the person of Christ, the last of the great patristic preachers had already passed from the scene—Basil the Great, Gregory of Nazianzus, Gregory of Nyssa, John Chrysostom, Theodore of Mopsuestia, Jerome, and Augustine of Hippo were dead.

During the next thousand years, known today as the Middle Ages, the church suffered a number of setbacks, though we should not ignore the sparks of divine grace and truth that illuminated this age nor gloss over the variety of preachers and theologians who labored in those times. In the East, the church fell under the shadow of Islam. In the West, medieval preachers faced significant obstacles in interpreting the Scriptures, not least of which was the loss of the knowledge of biblical Hebrew and Greek.[1] Despite notable work by Dominicans and Franciscans in the thirteenth century,[2] medieval preaching too often sank into neglect in favor of the ceremonial glory enveloping the liturgy of the church and the political glory elevating the papacy and its episcopal appendages.

---

1. Hughes Oliphant Old, *The Reading and Preaching of the Scriptures in the Worship of the Christian Church* (Grand Rapids: Eerdmans, 1998), 3:xvi. I thank Paul Smalley for his research assistance.

2. The Franciscan order was founded in 1209, and the Dominican in 1250. More than eighty thousand sermon manuscripts have been identified from the years 1150 to 1350. O. C. Edwards Jr., *A History of Preaching* (Nashville: Abingdon, 2004), 210–11.

In the sixteenth century, God visited European Christianity with a different kind of glory—the glory of the renewed preaching of Christ and Him crucified. The recovery of a right understanding of the gospel led to a renovation of preaching as the proclamation of Christ as the only Savior. Hughes Oliphant Old writes, "We would be terribly misled if we imagined that the Protestant Reformers rediscovered preaching. The Church in which the Reformers were born and brought up loved preaching…. What happened was that with the Reformation came a refocusing of preaching, a rethinking of its purpose and a reevaluation of its relation to the worship of the Church."[3] Preaching was recognized as the primary means by which God's sovereign grace in Christ works in His people. The hearing of the Word was exalted as an act of worship offered to God through Christ. As David L. Larsen notes, Scripture was released from the oppressive burden of conforming to ecclesiastical agendas, recovered its central position vis-à-vis the sacraments, and penetrated the culture afresh through the priesthood of all believers applied practically through the printing press.[4]

There is a mutual relation between the reformation of biblical doctrine and the revival of biblical preaching. Edwin C. Dargan wrote,

> The great events and achievements of that mighty revolution [i.e., the Reformation] were largely the work of preachers and preaching; for it was by the Word of God through the ministry of earnest men who believed, loved and taught it, that the best and most enduring work of the Reformation was done. And conversely, the events and principles of the movement powerfully reacted on preaching itself, giving it new spirit, new power, new forms.[5]

Thus Dargan concludes that in the sixteenth century "a distinctly new epoch in the history of preaching meets us now, and the greatest and most fruitful one since the fourth century."[6]

The result was a return to expository preaching—that is, to sermons developed out of the text of Scripture, as is evident in the massive corpus of

---

3. Old, *Reading and Preaching of the Scriptures*, 4:1.

4. David L. Larsen, *The Company of the Preachers: A History of Biblical Preaching from the Old Testament to the Modern Era* (Grand Rapids: Kregel, 1998), 142.

5. Edwin C. Dargan, *A History of Preaching* (repr., Grand Rapids: Baker, 1974), 1:366–67.

6. Dargan, *History of Preaching*, 1:367.

sermons by Martin Luther.[7] T. H. L. Parker observes, "In the Reformation preaching occupied a position which it had not since the fifth century. The gospel is a return through Augustine to the New Testament; the form [of the sermon] is a return to the homily of the Fathers."[8]

It would be profitable to give consideration to the preaching of Luther and his followers in the Lutheran or Augsburger tradition. However, for the purpose of this chapter, our focus must be limited to the Reformed or Calvinist preachers of the sixteenth century, and even here we will be selective. We will note some great characteristics of their preaching that are worthy of our imitation and adaptation today.

Reformed Expository Preaching

One of the greatest events of the Reformation happened in 1519, when Ulrich Zwingli (1484–1531) began his ministry as a preacher in the Grossmünster of Zurich with a series of sermons that worked through the gospel of Matthew. He popularized the method of *lectio continua*, what we today would call the sustained and systematic serial exposition of the text of the Scriptures.[9] Old describes Zwingli's preaching in this way:

> Zwingli was inspired by the *lectio continua* preaching of Chrysostom. He followed the system through his entire ministry, covering in succession Matthew, which took a whole year's worth of daily preaching, the Acts of the Apostles, 1 Timothy, the two epistles of Peter, and Hebrews. In 1524 he is known to have preached through the Gospel of John and then to have finished up the rest of the Pauline Epistles. After seven years of daily preaching he had treated most of the New Testament. He then turned to the Old Testament, preaching first the Psalms. Then he began the Pentateuch in the middle of July 1526. He seems to have continued through the Historical Books until March 1528, when he began Isaiah. Then he continued through the Prophets for some time—how long we do not know. This systematic interpretation of Scripture was received with considerable enthusiasm in Zurich, and his colleagues observed it with great interest. One by one the Christian humanist preachers of the

---

7. Dargan notes, "About twenty-three hundred of the more than four thousand sermons Luther preached are included in the twenty-two volumes devoted to them in the Weimar editions of his works." Dargan, *History of Preaching*, 294.

8. T. H. L Parker, *The Oracles of God: An Introduction to the Preaching of John Calvin* (London: Lutterworth Press, 1947), 20.

9. Old, *Reading and Preaching of the Scriptures*, 4:43.

Upper Rhineland began to follow his example. In southern Germany it was this kind of systematic biblical preaching which won the people to the Reformation.[10]

Zwingli believed that as God's Word, the Scriptures had both perspicuity, or clarity, and authority in themselves. He wrote, "When the Word of God shines on the human understanding, it enlightens it in such a way that it understands and confesses the Word and knows the certainty of it."[11] The Bible is self-authenticating, for it is the voice of God. The Word of God "comes with such clarity and assurance that it is surely known and believed."[12] This belief gave him confidence to preach the Scriptures alone, and not the ideas of men. He said: "No matter who a man may be, if he teaches you in accordance with his own thought and mind his teaching is false. But if he teaches you in accordance with the Word of God, it is not he that teaches you, but God who teaches him."[13] This approach put the preacher in the position of a humble servant under the authority of the Lord. After a near fatal bout of the plague in 1519, Zwingli wrote in prayer to God, "Do what Thou wilt," for "I am Thy tool, to make whole or break."[14]

Heinrich Bullinger (1504–1575) replaced Zwingli when the latter died in 1531. When Bullinger preached his first sermon in the Grossmünster of Zurich after Zwingli's death, people were overwhelmed with excitement. As Oswald Myconius (1488–1552) observed, "Bullinger thundered out such a sermon that many believed that Zwingli was not dead but, like the phoenix, has been raised again to life." As a result, Zurich quickly called Bullinger, who was only a visiting preacher, to be its minister.[15]

Bullinger's productivity in the pulpit was amazing. He preached through fifty-three of the sixty-six books of the Bible at least once. Some books he preached through twice (Isaiah, Daniel, Hosea, Amos, Nahum, Matthew,

---

10. Old, *Reading and Preaching of the Scriptures*, 4:46. As Old notes, Zwingli at times broke from his *lectio continua* and delivered messages for special occasions.

11. Ulrich Zwingli, *Of the Clarity and Certainty of the Word of God*, in *Zwingli and Bullinger*, ed. Geoffrey W. Bromiley, Library of Christian Classics 24 (Philadelphia: Westminster Press, 1953), 75.

12. Zwingli, *Clarity and Certainty*, 77.

13. Zwingli, *Clarity and Certainty*, 90.

14. As quoted in Lee Palmer Wandel, "Zwingli, Huldrych," *The Oxford Encyclopedia of the Reformation* (Oxford: Oxford University Press, 1996), 4:321.

15. Walter Hollweg, *Heinrich Bullingers Hausbuch: Eine Untersuchung Über Die Anfänge Der Reformierten Predigtliteratur* (Neukirchen, Kreis Moers: Verlag der Buchhandlung des Erziehungsvereins, 1956), 18–19.

Mark, Paul's epistles, and 2 Peter); some, three times (Joel, Obadiah, Jonah, Habakkuk, Zephaniah, Haggai, Zechariah, Malachi, Luke, John, Acts, 1 Peter, and 1 John); and at least one, four times (Hebrews).

Bullinger also wrote thirteen volumes of commentaries that covered the entire New Testament except for Revelation. Later, however, he published one hundred sermons on Revelation. He also published sermons on some books from the Old Testament. He wrote 170 sermons on Jeremiah, 66 sermons on Daniel, and 190 sermons on Isaiah. In all, he published 618 sermons, but none of them became as popular as those that were collected as *The Decades*.

We find another example of expository preaching through books of the Bible in the French Reformer of Geneva, John Calvin (1509–1564). Calvin preached serially from various books of the Bible, striving to show the meaning of a passage and how it should impact the lives of his hearers. Much like ancient church homilies in style, his sermons had no divisions or points other than what the text dictated. As Paul T. Fuhrmann writes, "They are properly homilies as in the ancient church: expositions of Bible passages [in] the light of grammar and history, [providing] application to the hearers' life situations."[16]

Calvin was a careful exegete, an able expositor, and faithful in applying the Word. His goals in preaching were to glorify God, to cause believers to grow in the grace and in the knowledge of Christ Jesus, and to unite sinners with Christ so "that men be reconciled to God by the free remission of sins."[17] This aim of saving sinners blended seamlessly with his emphasis on scriptural doctrines. He wrote that ministers are "keepers of the truth of God."[18] Calvin frequently admonished ministers to keep this treasure safe by handling the Word of God carefully, always striving for the purest biblical teaching. That concern did not exclude bringing the Word to bear on contemporary events in people's lives, however. As current events related to the passage being expounded, Calvin felt free to apply his sermon to those events in practical, experiential, and moral ways.[19]

In England, William Perkins (1558–1602) embraced the Reformation emphasis on the exposition of Scripture but developed a more structured

---

16. Paul T. Fuhrmann, "Calvin, Expositor of Scripture," *Interpretation* 6, no. 2 (April 1952): 191.

17. John Calvin, *Commentaries* (1844–1856; repr., Grand Rapids: Baker, 1996), on John 20:23.

18. John Calvin, *The Mystery of Godliness* (Grand Rapids: Eerdmans, 1950), 122.

19. A. Mitchell Hunter, "Calvin as a Preacher," *Expository Times* 30, no. 12 (September 1919): 563.

style of expounding and applying the doctrines of the biblical text. He viewed preaching as crucial to the ministry of the church, being the instrument by which God implements His election of sinners to salvation in Christ.[20] Detesting the substitution of eloquence for biblical preaching, Perkins led the Puritan movement to reform preaching. He did so by his instruction to theological students at Cambridge; in his manual on preaching, *The Arte of Prophecying* (Latin 1592, English 1606), which quickly became a classic among Puritans; in advocating a method and plain style of preaching in his own pulpit exercises; and, above all, by stressing the experiential application of the doctrine of predestination.

Joseph A. Pipa Jr. suggests three reasons why Perkins wrote his preaching manual. First, there was a "dearth of able preachers in Elizabethan England."[21] Despite calls for the training of preachers as early as the time of William Tyndale (d. 1536), by 1583 only one-sixth of English clergy were licensed to preach, and even in 1603 there were only half as many preachers as parishes. Second, there were gaps in the university curriculum, with particular deficiencies in regard to theology, preaching, and spiritual direction. Perkins wrote his textbook to help fill the gap in practical theology. Third, Perkins aimed to promote a "plain" style of preaching as opposed to the ornate and literary style of High-Church Anglicans.[22] The latter style heaped up quotations from ancient authorities, often in Greek or Latin, together with many puns, extravagant and surprising analogies, rhymes, and alliteration. Such "witty" preachers sought to please the ear with art and to impress the mind with philosophy. This style went hand in hand with the belief that grace came primarily through the sacraments, in contrast to the Puritan emphasis on preaching as the primary and central means of grace.[23]

Perkins's model of preaching influenced generations to come. Ian Breward confirms this influence when he writes of Perkins, "His emphasis on simplicity in preaching and his advocacy of a sermon structured according to

---

20. Joel R. Beeke, "William Perkins on Predestination, Preaching, and Conversion," in *The Practical Calvinist*, ed. Peter A. Lillback (Fearn, Ross-shire, Scotland: Christian Focus, 2002), 183–213.

21. Joseph A. Pipa Jr., "William Perkins and the Development of Puritan Preaching" (PhD diss., Westminster Theological Seminary, 1985), 86.

22. Pipa, "William Perkins and the Development of Puritan Preaching," 87–88.

23. See Pipa, "William Perkins and the Development of Puritan Preaching," 37–42.

doctrine, reason and use was taken for granted as homiletic orthodoxy until the end of the seventeenth century and beyond."[24]

Perkins's approach to preaching was shaped by the doctrines of the Reformation. First, Perkins set forth a high view of the Word of God. It is sufficient, that is, "so complete, that nothing may be either put to it, or taken from it, which appertaineth to the proper end thereof." It is pure, or "void of deceit and error." It is authoritative as "the supreme and absolute determination of the controversies of the church ought to be given unto it." The Word is powerful, able to search and discern the heart of man and to bind the conscience. "The Scripture is the word of God written...by men immediately called to be the clerks or secretaries of the Holy Ghost." The sum of its message is the incarnate Christ and His saving work. Therefore, the preacher must confine himself to the Holy Scriptures for the matter of his sermons, and insofar as he does so, his preaching is "the voice of God."[25]

Second, Perkins called preachers to study the Scriptures both accurately and wisely. Much of his preaching manual sets forth principles of biblical interpretation. His method of interpretation is (1) *theological*, built upon a fundamental knowledge of Christian doctrine as summarized in the Apostles' Creed, the Ten Commandments, and other formulations; (2) *broadly biblical*, viewing any one text in the light of the teaching of the whole Bible, especially in key books such as Romans, the gospel of John, Psalms, Isaiah, and Genesis; (3) *historical*, rooting our interpretations on the writings of the church through the ages that the preacher must ever be reading; (4) *prayerful*, asking God to open the preacher's eyes (Ps. 119:18), for "the principal interpreter of the Scripture is the Holy Ghost"; (5) *literal and grammatical*, seeking the natural sense of the words and sentences and avoiding fanciful, mystical, or allegorical readings; (6) *contextual*, asking questions about the writers and the setting of the text; and (7) *rhetorical*, recognizing figures of speech such as metaphors, irony, or theanthropism, namely, speaking of God by analogy to human nature or qualities.[26] Such principles all aim at "the opening of the words and sentences of the Scripture, that one entire and natural sense may appear."[27]

---

24. Ian Breward, ed., *The Work of William Perkins*, The Courtenay Library of Reformation Classics (Abingdon, England: Sutton Courtenay Press, 1970), 112.

25. William Perkins, *The Arte of Prophecying*, in *The Workes of that Famous and Worthy Minister of Christ, in the Universitie of Cambridge, M. William Perkins* (London: John Legat, 1609), 2:731–32.

26. Perkins, *Arte of Prophecying*, 2:736–49.

27. Perkins, *Arte of Prophecying*, 2:737.

Third, Perkins instructed preachers to crystallize the meaning of the Scripture text into doctrinal propositions or distinct teachings. Many texts clearly express a doctrine. In other texts, the preacher may infer or deduce doctrines through sound reasoning and logic. The examples of biblical characters can point to principles applicable to someone in a similar position in the family, the government, or the church. Doctrines derived from the Bible "by just consequence" should be confirmed by a few testimonies from other Scripture passages, but merely human testimonies do not have the authority to prove a point.[28]

Finally, Perkins said, "Christ is the substance or subject matter of the whole Bible."[29] He wrote: "Christ stands alone in the work of redemption, without colleague or partner, without deputy or substitute, whether we respect the whole work of redemption, or the least part of it." Perkins affirmed with Peter that "there is no other name under heaven given among men by which we must be saved" (Acts 4:12), and with Paul that Christ "is also able to save to the uttermost those who come to God through Him" (Heb. 7:25). In Him we are complete (Col. 2:10).[30] Perkins said that the heart of all preaching is "to preach one Christ, by Christ, to the praise of Christ."[31]

Reformed Experiential Preaching

The Reformers promoted experiential, or "experimental," Christianity. Calvin paraphrased Psalm 27:9 this way: "Make me truly to experience that thou hast been near to me, and let me clearly behold thy power in saving me." He then commented, "We must observe the distinction between the theoretical knowledge derived from the Word of God and what is called the experimental knowledge of his grace." The latter knowledge is imparted when "God shows himself present in operation," but "he must first be sought in his Word."[32] Thus, Calvin believed that the objective truth of Scripture is foundational

---

28. Perkins, *Arte of Prophecying*, 2:750–51. On Perkins's commendation at this point of Ramist methods of logic for the interpretation of Scripture, see Wilbur Samuel Howell, *Logic and Rhetoric in England, 1500–1700* (New York: Russell and Russell, 1961), 206–7.

29. William Perkins, *A Commentary, Or, Exposition upon the Five First Chapters of the Epistle to the Galatians*, in *The Works of William Perkins*, ed. Paul M. Smalley (Grand Rapids: Reformation Heritage Books, 2015), 2:58 (on Gal. 1:15–17). Henceforth *Commentary on Galatians*.

30. Perkins, *Commentary on Galatians*, 2:272 (on Gal. 4:8–11).

31. Perkins, *Arte of Prophecying*, 2:762.

32. Calvin, *Commentaries*, on Ps. 27:9.

to Christianity, but that truth must also become "experimental knowledge," that is, knowledge of the truth by personal experience.

Commenting on David's outcry in Psalm 33:19, Calvin wrote that "David not only asserts that God is good, but…is ravished with admiration of the goodness which he had experienced." There is an experience that only believers can know because it is the exercise of a new spiritual sense. The goodness of God fills the world, yet it is hidden to unbelievers, being reserved to "the experience of the saints, because they alone, as I have said, experience in their souls the fruit of divine goodness."[33]

This is not to say that faith and experience are two different things. Rather, faith is the root of experience and experience is the fruition of faith. Thus, Calvin wrote of "the gracious experience of faith."[34] He also says that experiential knowledge "makes the deepest impression."[35] Relying on God means that "we embrace with our whole hearts" the promises of God's grace and "endeavor to have the experience of his goodness pervading our whole minds." Then we are prepared to stand firm with strength in the face of our daily conflicts.[36]

In order to promote the experiential Christian life, the Reformers aimed to deliver sermons that were faithfully applicatory, spiritually discriminating, and powerfully authoritative. We will examine each of these aspects of their preaching in turn.

Applicatory Preaching

Theodore Beza (1519–1605) was Calvin's successor in Geneva. Beza's preaching has been neglected by scholars, who tend to focus on his writings with regard to predestination. However, Scott M. Manetsch has shown that preaching played a central role in Beza's ministry in Geneva. He writes, "From the time he arrived in Geneva in the fall of 1558, until poor health finally forced him to step down permanently from the pulpit in 1600, Beza may have preached as many as four thousand sermons to his congregation at St. Pierre's."[37]

---

33. Calvin, *Commentaries*, on Ps. 31:19.

34. Calvin, *Commentaries*, on Ps. 36:8.

35. Calvin, *Commentaries*, on Ps. 66:5. The French version reads "cognoissance d'experience et de prattique" (knowledge of experience and practice).

36. Calvin, *Commentaries*, on Ps. 31:24.

37. Scott M. Manetsch, "*Onus Praedicandi*: The Preaching Ministry of Theodore Beza" (unpublished paper, Calvin College and Seminary, n.d.), 1. I am indebted to Manetch's

As Manetsch notes, Beza understood the calling of a pastor to be the imparting of knowledge, not in the manner of a theological professor but as a shepherd caring for his sheep.[38] Beza wrote,

> At all times, the prophets, Jesus Christ and the Apostles spoke ever and only in the language of the common people, so that they were understood by every man in their nation.... We say, and practice thus, that the pastors must feed their flock with the Word of Life, and that the sheep, on their side, should know and understand that which is proclaimed to them, in order to be nourished and consoled by it, and in order to be put on their guard against the wolves and false prophets.[39]

Preachers aim to apply truth to living souls of human beings whom they know by name.[40] Beza said, "But pastors must go further [than teaching doctrine]. For, in preaching, they apply the doctrine to the needs of the Church, to teach, to rebuke, to console and exhort in public and in private, according to the need.... They also make public prayer. In brief, they watch day and night over their flock whom they feed in public and in private with the Word of life (Acts 20:20)."[41]

Beza himself practiced a very direct and applied form of preaching. Manetsch writes: "In his pulpit ministry, therefore, we see Beza functioning as exegete, theologian, social commentator, personal counselor, and public information director. Far from being elegant or speculative, Beza's preaching is direct and passionate, intended to excite interest, instill conviction, and compel change in his audience."[42] In fact, his denunciation of the sins of Geneva and its spiritual apathy sometimes stirred the resentment of both church members and the civil magistrates.[43]

Drawing lines between right and wrong and sounding the trumpet of warning against sin requires courage and discernment. Beza described the calling of a faithful preacher against sin as follows:

---

research, much of which is included in his book *Calvin's Company of Preachers: Pastoral Care and the Emerging Reformed Church, 1536–1609* (Oxford: Oxford University Press, 2012).

38. Manetsch, "*Onus Praedicandi*: The Preaching Ministry of Theodore Beza," 8.

39. Theodore Beza, *The Christian Faith*, trans. James Clark (Lewes: Focus Christian Ministries Trust, 1992), iv.

40. Manetsch, "*Onus Praedicandi*: The Preaching Ministry of Theodore Beza," 8.

41. Beza, *Christian Faith*, 93 (5.26).

42. Manetsch, "*Onus Praedicandi*: The Preaching Ministry of Theodore Beza," 12.

43. Manetsch, "*Onus Praedicandi*: The Preaching Ministry of Theodore Beza," 13–14.

If he wants to please men, he is no longer a servant of God (Gal. 1:10). Therefore after knowledge he will ask God first for a spirit of discretion not to reprove anything lightly without knowing and understanding the fact that he is reproving. Next he will ask for the true use of the language of God, not just to speak, but to speak frankly as one must speak (Eph. 6:20). And closing his ear to threats and all respect for persons, he should listen to the Lord who is admonishing him in the manner of Isaiah, "Proclaim it with a full voice, do not spare yourself, raise up your voice like a horn and declare their trespasses to my people, and declare their sins to the house of Jacob [Isa. 58:1]."[44]

At the same time, he understood that mere words, no matter how true, are insufficient to overcome man's natural blindness. Even believers need more grace to know the truth rightly as they should. He wrote, "But we, my brothers, who are of the number of those to whom God gave the grace of calling them from darkness into so admirable a light (1 Peter 2:9)…let us learn to ask our God for an increase of this true sense of his light."[45] He exhorted men to pray for inward spiritual light and heat: "We must ask the Lord that he change and correct [our reason], even as dead as it is with regard to that truth (Eph. 2:1), he gives us life, by giving us movement and affection from the beginning until the end." Even those who have "eyes of faith" see at best "bleary-eyed or completely one-eyed."[46]

With a true experiential balance, Beza called for a Christianity that is real both in the heart and in the conduct. He said: "The Lord does not want only that we believe, but he wants us to believe from the heart.… Never will a man be recognized as a Christian before God, unless he believes inwardly and shows it clearly on the outside."[47]

Discriminating Preaching

Another approach to faithful application is to consider the spiritual condition of those who hear the sermon. Perkins schematized listeners into seven categories.[48] His analysis reflects what we call discriminating preaching, that

---

44. Beza, "Sermon," in Shawn D. Wright, *Our Sovereign Refuge: The Pastoral Theology of Theodore Beza* (Carlisle, U.K.: Paternoster, 2004), 246–47.

45. Beza, "Sermon," 249.

46. Beza, "Sermon," 250–51.

47. Beza, "Sermon," 251.

48. Perkins, *Arte of Prophecying*, 2:752–56.

is, sermons that give distinct applications aimed at different spiritual conditions. The listeners may fall into several categories:

1. *Ignorant and unteachable unbelievers.* These people need to hear
   the doctrine of the Word in clear, reasonable teaching as well as by
   reproof aimed at pricking of their consciences.

2. *Ignorant but teachable unbelievers.* These people must be taught
   the foundational doctrines of the Christian religion. As a help, Perkins recommended his book *Foundations of the Christian Religion*,
   which covers the subjects of repentance, faith, the sacraments,
   application of the Word, the resurrection, and the last judgment.

3. *Those who have some knowledge but are not humbled.* To them, the
   preacher must especially proclaim the law to stir up sorrow and
   repentance for sin, followed by the preaching of the gospel.

4. *The humbled.* The preacher must not give comfort to such people
   too soon but must first determine whether their humility results
   from God's saving work rooted in faith or from mere common
   conviction. To the partly humbled, who are not yet stripped of
   self-righteousness, Perkins says that the law must be propounded
   yet the more, albeit tempered with the gospel, so that "being terrified with their sins, and with the meditation of God's judgment,
   they may together also at the same instant receive solace by the
   gospel." To the fully humbled, "the doctrine of faith and repentance, and the comforts of the gospel ought to be promulged
   [proclaimed] and tendered."[49]

5. *Those who believe.* Believers need to be taught the key doctrines of
   justification, sanctification, and perseverance, along with the law
   as the rule of life or conduct for Christians rather than as a sting
   and curse to sinners. Before faith, the law with its curse is to be
   preached; after conversion, the law without the curse.

6. *Those who are fallen, either in faith or in practice.* These people
   have declined in faith, in knowledge, or in apprehending Christ.
   If they have failed in knowledge, they are to be instructed in the
   particular doctrine from which they have erred. If they fail to

---

49. Perkins, *Arte of Prophecying*, 2:754–55.

apprehend Christ, they should examine themselves by the marks of grace, then fly to Christ as the remedy of the gospel. Those who fall in practice have become involved in sinful behavior. They need to be brought to repentance by the preaching of the law and the gospel.

7. *A mixed group.* This may refer to the mixture of both believers and unbelievers in a church, or it may refer to individuals who contain within themselves a combination of the traits of the first six kinds of listeners. If the latter is what Perkins intends, much wisdom is needed to know how much law and how much gospel to bring to them. In either case, the wise preacher knows that he is nearly always addressing a "mixed multitude."

Authoritative Preaching

Though realistic in their view of ministry, the Reformers had great expectations for what God can do through a Spirit-anointed preacher of the Word. Calvin called the preaching office "the most excellent of all things," commended by God that it might be held in the highest esteem. "There is nothing more notable or glorious in the church than the ministry of the gospel," he concluded.[50] In commenting on Isaiah 55:11, he said, "The Word goeth out of the mouth of God in such a manner that it likewise goeth out of the mouth of men; for God does not speak openly from heaven but employs men as his instruments."[51]

Calvin viewed preaching as God's ordinary means of salvation and benediction. He said that the Holy Spirit is the "internal minister" who uses the "external minister" in preaching the Word. The external minister "holds forth the vocal word and it is received by the ears," but the internal minister "truly communicates the thing proclaimed [which] is Christ."[52] Thus, God Himself speaks through the mouths of His servants by His Spirit. "Wherever the gospel is preached, it is as if God himself came into the midst of us," Calvin wrote.[53] Preaching is the instrument and the authoritative word

---

50. John Calvin, *Institutes of the Christian Religion*, trans. Ford Lewis Battles, ed. John T. McNeill (Philadelphia: Westminster Press, 1960), 4.3.3.

51. Calvin, *Commentaries*, on Isa. 55:11.

52. John Calvin, *Tracts and Treatises*, trans. Henry Beveridge (Grand Rapids: Eerdmans, 1958), 1:173.

53. Calvin, *Commentaries*, on Matt. 24:14.

that the Spirit uses in His saving work of illuminating, converting, and seal-
ing sinners. "There is…an inward efficacy of the Holy Spirit when he sheds
forth his power upon hearers, that they may embrace a discourse [sermon]
by faith."[54]

Perkins similarly advised preachers to deliver their sermons with Spirit-
worked liberty, sincerity, and power. He recommended that the preacher
memorize an outline of his sermon and not be concerned about the specific
choice of words. The minister should modestly conceal his scholarship but
preach with the demonstration of the Spirit (1 Cor. 2:1–5).[55] He explained,
"The demonstration of the Spirit is, when as the minister of the Word doth
in the time of preaching behave himself, that all, even ignorant persons and
unbelievers may judge that it is not him that speaketh, as the Spirit of God
in him and by him."[56] Spiritual preaching speaks with simplicity, clarity, the
fear of God's majesty, and love for the people. It avoids unnecessary use of
technical language as well as entertaining stories and jesting. Instead, it dis-
plays dignity, seriousness, ability to teach, authority as God's message, and
"zeal, whereby being most desirous of God's glory he doth endeavor to fulfill
and execute the decree of election concerning the salvation of men by his
ministry."[57] In the hands of the Holy Spirit, the preacher is an instrument for
the execution of the decree of divine election.

A Heritage of Preaching through the Centuries

Although sermonic style varies in different times and places, the Reformation produced a legacy of expositional and experiential preaching that godly
men have passed down through the ages. This was certainly the case among
the seventeenth-century Puritans.[58] It continued among preachers in various
branches of the Reformation tradition, including Presbyterians, Anglicans,
Congregationalists, and Baptists. Princeton's Archibald Alexander (1772–
1851) said, "The word of God should be so handled, that it may be adapted
to Christians in different states and stages of the divine life; for while some
Christians are like 'strong men,' others are but 'babes in Christ, who must be

---

54. Calvin, *Commentaries*, on Ezek. 1:3.
55. Perkins, *Arte of Prophecying*, 2:758–59.
56. Perkins, *Arte of Prophecying*, 2:759.
57. Perkins, *Arte of Prophecying*, 2:761.
58. Joel R. Beeke and Mark Jones, *A Puritan Theology: Doctrine for Life* (Grand Rapids:
Reformation Heritage Books, 2012), 681–710.

fed with milk, and not with strong meat.'"[59] Alexander went on to explain how the Reformed preacher also should "rightly divide" the Word by making specific applications to the backsliding, the worldly minded, the afflicted, and the dying believer.[60] Anglican Charles Bridges (1794–1869) called for perpetual application throughout the sermon and for preaching that drew clear lines between different spiritual conditions and states, addressing the needs of people in each case.[61]

Until the mid-nineteenth century, many Reformed ministers continued to preach experientially. Looking back on his life among the Baptists, Francis Wayland (1796–1865) recalled,

> From the manner in which our ministers entered upon the work, it is evident that it must have been the prominent object of their lives to convert men to God.... They were remarkable for what was called experimental preaching. They told much of the exercises of the human soul under the influence of the truth of the gospel:
>
> - the feeling of a sinner while under the convicting power of the truth;
> - the various subterfuges to which he resorted when aware of his danger;
> - the successive applications of truth by which he was driven out of all of them;
> - the despair of the soul when it found itself wholly without a refuge;
> - its final submission to God, and simple reliance on Christ;
> - the joys of the new birth and the earnestness of the soul to introduce others to the happiness which it has now for the first time experienced;
> - the trials of the soul when it found itself an object of reproach and persecution among those whom it loved best;
> - the process of sanctification;
> - the devices of Satan to lead us into sin;

---

59. Archibald Alexander, "Rightly Dividing the Word of Truth," in *The Princeton Pulpit*, ed. John T. Duffield (New York: Charles Scribner, 1852), 42.

60. Alexander, "Rightly Dividing the Word of Truth," 42–45.

61. Charles Bridges, *The Christian Ministry* (London: Banner of Truth, 2006), 277.

- the mode in which the attacks of the adversary may be resisted;

- the danger of backsliding, with its evidences, and the means of recovery from it.

Wayland concludes with these sad words: "These remarks show the tendency of the class of preachers which seems now to be passing away."[62]

Though many preachers today are ignorant of the experiential wealth of their Reformed homiletical heritage, there are encouraging signs of the rise of preachers, such as my good friend Steven Lawson, who stand in the same great tradition as Zwingli, Bullinger, Calvin, Beza, and Perkins. May God grant that the legacy of Reformed expositional and experiential preaching be recovered in this generation with fresh invigoration from the Holy Spirit, that it may be a means of reviving God's church, awakening our careless nations, and gathering many lost souls to Jesus Christ.

---

62. Francis Wayland, *Notes on the Principles and Practices of Baptist Churches* (New York: Sheldon, Blakeman, and Co., 1857), 40–43. I have separated Wayland's paragraph into bullet points for easier reading.

PART 2

The Meaning of Preaching

CHAPTER 5

Preaching as Exposition

R. Albert Mohler Jr.

The preaching of the Word is central, irreducible, and nonnegotiable to authentic worship that pleases God. John Stott's simple declaration states the issue boldly: "Preaching is indispensable to Christianity."

More specifically, preaching is indispensable to Christian worship. But if preaching is central to Christian worship, what kind of preaching are we talking about? The sheer weightlessness of much contemporary preaching is a severe indictment of our superficial Christianity. When the pulpit ministry lacks substance, the church is severed from the Word of God, and its health and faithfulness are immediately diminished.

The preaching that is central to Christian worship is expository preaching—that is, preaching that always derives its message from a passage of the Bible. In fact, the only form of authentic Christian preaching is expository preaching.

A Crisis in Preaching

One of the hallmarks of our time is that we face a crisis in preaching. Indeed, it would be an exercise in self-delusion if we tried to pretend that nothing is wrong with the preaching that happens in most evangelical churches. Let me ask some honest and difficult questions: If you picked an evangelical church at random and attended a Sunday morning service there, how likely is it that you would hear a faithful expository sermon, one that takes its message and its structure from the biblical text? If you answer that question honestly, you will admit that your expectation would not be high. Further, do you believe that as time passes it is becoming more likely or less likely that you would hear an expository message in that random church?

I am convinced that we add to the confusion by discussing expository preaching as merely one kind of preaching—or even the best kind. When we fall into that pattern, we do serious injury to the scriptural vision of preaching. Let's be clear. According to the Bible, exposition is preaching, and preaching is exposition.

Here we must deal not only with what preaching really is but also with what it is not. Much of what happens in pulpits across America today is not preaching, even though the preacher—and probably his congregation along with him—would claim that it is. Preaching is not the task of saying something interesting about God, nor is it delivering a religious discourse or narrating a story.

Many evangelicals are seduced by the proponents of topical and narrative preaching that does not focus on explaining the Scripture. The declarative force of Scripture is blunted by a demand for story, and the textual shape of the Bible is supplanted by man-centered topical considerations. In many pulpits, the Bible, if referenced at all, becomes merely a source for pithy aphorisms or convenient narratives. Moreover, the therapeutic concerns of the culture too often set the agenda for evangelical preaching. Issues of the self predominate, and the congregation expects to hear simple answers to complex problems. The essence of most therapeutic preaching comes down to an affirmation of the self and its importance. Evangelicals, much like their secular neighbors, now represent the age of "psychological man." The "triumph of the therapeutic" hits close to home when evangelicals are honest about the preaching they want to hear and expect to receive.

Furthermore, postmodernism claims intellectual primacy in the culture, and even if many Americans do not surrender entirely to doctrinal relativism, they allow and demand moral autonomy and a minimum of intellectual and moral requirements. The average congregant expects to make his or her own final decisions about all the important issues of life, from worldview to lifestyle.

However, the solid truth of Christianity stands in stark contrast to these flimsy pretensions of postmodernity. As theologian David F. Wells notes, "Sustaining orthodoxy and framing Christian belief in doctrinal terms requires habits of reflection and judgment that are simply out of place in our culture and increasingly are disappearing from evangelicalism as well."[1]

---

1. David F. Wells, *No Place for Truth, or Whatever Happened to Evangelical Theology?* (Grand Rapids: Eerdmans, 1993), 173.

Consequently, the appetite for serious preaching has virtually disappeared among many Christians, who are content to have their fascinations with themselves encouraged from the pulpit.

One reason for our modern confusion is that many preachers would claim that their preaching is expository, even though this often means no more than that the preacher has a biblical text in mind, no matter how tenuous may be the actual relationship between the text and the sermon. One of the first steps to a recovery of authentic Christian preaching is to stop saying, "I prefer expository preaching." Rather, we should define exactly what we mean when we say "preach." What we mean is, very simply, reading the text and explaining it—reproving, rebuking, exhorting, and patiently teaching directly from the text of Scripture. If a preacher is not doing that, then he is not preaching.

No better portrait of expository preaching can be found than Nehemiah 8:8. After the people gather at the Water Gate and demand that "the book" be brought forward, the text says of Ezra and his fellow scribes that "they read distinctly from the book, in the Law of God; and they gave the sense, and helped them to understand the reading." "Giving the sense" is not merely the act of translating from one language to another. It has to do with explaining a text, breaking it down, and making its meaning clear to the congregation. Essentially, this is what it means to preach. The heart and soul of expository preaching—of any true Christian preaching—is reading the Word of God and then explaining it to the people so that they understand it.

Deuteronomy 4 and Expository Preaching

If we are to recover authentic preaching of God's Word, one of the most important tasks facing us is to articulate a theology of expository preaching. Deuteronomy 4 is a good place to begin, for it is there that God speaks to His people and reminds them what it is that makes them unique among the peoples of the earth. What He says has direct relevance to expository preaching:

> "For ask now concerning the days that are past, which were before you, since the day that God created man on the earth, and ask from one end of heaven to the other, whether any great thing like this has happened, or anything like it has been heard. Did any people ever hear the voice of God speaking out of the midst of the fire, as you have heard, and live? Or did God ever try to go and take for Himself a nation from the midst of another nation, by trials, by signs, by wonders, by war, by a mighty

hand and an outstretched arm, and by great terrors, according to all that the LORD your God did for you in Egypt before your eyes? To you it was shown, that you might know that the LORD Himself is God; there is none other besides Him. Out of heaven He let you hear His voice, that He might instruct you; on earth He showed you His great fire, and you heard His words out of the midst of the fire. And because He loved your fathers, therefore He chose their descendants after them; and He brought you out of Egypt with His Presence, with His mighty power, driving out from before you nations greater and mightier than you, to bring you in, to give you their land as an inheritance, as it is this day. Therefore know this day, and consider it in your heart, that the LORD Himself is God in heaven above and on the earth beneath; there is no other. You shall therefore keep His statutes and His commandments which I command you today, that it may go well with you and with your children after you, and that you may prolong your days in the land which the LORD your God is giving you for all time." (Deut. 4:32–40)

The historical setting of this passage is important. The children of Israel are in the wilderness, and Moses is preparing them to enter the Land of Promise. Behind them is the entire history of the exodus from Egypt and the forty years of wandering in the desert—the giving of the law at Sinai and Horeb and the rebellion at Kadesh Barnea. They stood now on the bank of the Jordan River, and on the other side was the Promised Land.

In the great sermons that comprise the book of Deuteronomy, the Lord is speaking to His people through Moses so that they would be prepared for the challenge that lay before them. The book is called *Deutero-nomos* because it is a second giving of the law. As Moses lays the Lord's commands before the people yet again, they have another opportunity to be faithful rather than faithless, obedient rather than disobedient when they face their enemies in the Land of Promise. Would they be ready?

Notice that even as it is a book of preparation, Deuteronomy is not primarily a military briefing. It is not primarily about demographics and geography. Above all, it is about the word of God. It is about the fact that God has spoken, and His people need to be ready to hear Him and obey. The intensity here is enormous because the necessity of obedience is a matter of survival for Israel. The entire theology of Deuteronomy comes down to the fact that God has spoken. Thus, hearing and obeying is life, but refusing to hear and disobeying is death. Moses wants the people of Israel to know that life and death hang in the balance of their willingness to hear God's word and respond to it. It is a matter of life or death.

The central problem in our crisis of preaching today is that we think somehow that this has changed. We no longer believe that hearing and responding to the word of God is a matter of crucial importance. That is the only plausible reason I can offer for why expositional preaching is in decline, or is even absent, in so many pulpits. Before the decline in expository preaching, there was the abandonment of the conviction that the word of God comes as a matter of life and death.

Developing a Passion for Expository Preaching

The situation, however, is not irrecoverable—not if we regain a conviction that our spiritual lives and the life of the church itself depend on hearing and responding to the word of God in Scripture. Let's consider three things that we learn from Deuteronomy 4 that can help us to develop both a theology of and a passion for expository preaching.

First, *the only true and living God is the God who speaks.* We know who God is not because any of us was smart enough to figure Him out but because out of His own love, grace, and mercy He has spoken to us. Moses says this explicitly in Deuteronomy 4:35: "To you it was shown, that you might know that the LORD Himself is God; there is none other besides Him." The Israelites would not have known God at all unless He had spoken to them. This is the miracle of revelation, and I fear that we give this doctrine inadequate attention in our churches through our teaching and preaching. Instead of recognizing God's speaking to us in Scripture as a miracle of grace, we treat it as of little account. Instead of preaching the Word of God, we preach pop psychology and culture or we tell compelling stories. In Deuteronomy 4:10–19, Moses makes clear to the people of Israel that their lives depended on hearing and obeying God's word, which they must teach to their children and grandchildren,

> "especially concerning the day you stood before the LORD your God in Horeb, when the LORD said to me, 'Gather the people to Me, and I will let them hear My words, that they may learn to fear Me all the days they live on the earth, and that they may teach their children.'

> "Then you came near and stood at the foot of the mountain, and the mountain burned with fire to the midst of heaven, with darkness, cloud, and thick darkness. And the LORD spoke to you out of the midst of the

fire. You heard the sound of the words, but saw no form; you only heard a voice. So He declared to you His covenant which He commanded you to perform, the Ten Commandments; and He wrote them on two tablets of stone. And the LORD commanded me at that time to teach you statutes and judgments, that you might observe them in the land which you cross over to possess.

"Take careful heed to yourselves, for you saw no form when the LORD spoke to you at Horeb out of the midst of the fire, lest you act corruptly and make for yourselves a carved image in the form of any figure: the likeness of male or female, the likeness of any animal that is on the earth or the likeness of any winged bird that flies in the air, the likeness of anything that creeps on the ground or the likeness of any fish that is in the water beneath the earth. And take heed, lest you lift your eyes to heaven, and when you see the sun, the moon, and the stars, all the host of heaven, you feel driven to worship them and serve them, which the LORD your God has given to all the peoples under the whole heaven as a heritage." (Deut. 4:10–19)

Notice how Moses lovingly reminds the people that *they were there* when God spoke. "You came near," he says. "Do you remember how you stood at the foot of the mountain? Do you remember when you heard the voice of God speaking from the midst of the fire? You heard God's voice!"

Then, more pointedly in verse 15, he says, "You saw no form." You didn't see God. You heard Him. That was different from the pagan idols that surrounded Israel, and it showed them that their God was the only true and living God. The pagans could see their idols. They could even speak to them. But the pagans' idols never spoke. They were silent. That is the grand distinction made in the Old Testament over and over again between the true God and the false idols. The pagan peoples see their gods and speak to their gods; but the one true and living God is never seen, yet He speaks to His people.

Elijah used this truth when he confronted the pagan priests at Mount Carmel. First Kings 18:26–29 recounts the story:

So they took the bull which was given them, and they prepared it, and called on the name of Baal from morning even till noon, saying, "O Baal, hear us!" But there was no voice; no one answered. Then they leaped about the altar which they had made.

And so it was, at noon, that Elijah mocked them and said, "Cry aloud, for he is a god; either he is meditating, or he is busy, or he is on a journey, or perhaps he is sleeping and must be awakened." So they cried aloud, and cut themselves, as was their custom, with knives and lances, until the blood gushed out on them. And when midday was past, they prophesied until the time of the offering of the evening sacrifice. But there was no voice; no one answered, no one paid attention.

What a haunting passage! Despite all the frantic dancing and blood-letting, "there was no voice; no one answered." In response to all the raving by those pagan priests, "no one answered, no one paid attention."

Jeremiah similarly says of the pagan idols, "They are upright, like a palm tree, and they cannot speak" (Jer. 10:5). And Paul tells his readers in 1 Corinthians 12:2, "You know that you were…carried away to these dumb idols, however you were led." Throughout Scripture, the contrast is pressed between the mute, dumb idols that sit like scarecrows in a cucumber field and the one, living, *speaking* God. This reminds us again of the gift of revelation, God's forfeiting of His own personal privacy, as Carl Henry put it. Stop and think about that. The God who needs nothing, sovereign in His majesty and infinite in His perfections, decided to reveal Himself to us so we might know Him. If that is true, then wouldn't you think that a people who are the recipients of such a gift would live by it, hunger for it, and cling to it?

I fear that there are many evangelicals today who believe that God *spoke* but doubt whether He *speaks*. They know and talk about the fact that God spoke in the Old Testament but think now that He no longer does so and that they must therefore invent new ways to convince people to love Him. But if you are a preacher of God's Word and you think that all of God's speaking was in the past, then resign. I say that with deadly seriousness. If you do not believe that God now speaks from His Word—the Bible—then what are you doing every Sunday morning? If you are not confident that God speaks as you rightly read and explain the Word of God, then you should quit.

But if you do believe that—if you truly believe that God speaks through His Word—then why would you substitute anything else in place of the expository preaching of the Bible? What is more important for your people than to hear from God, and how else is that going to happen unless you, like Ezra, open the book, read it, and explain it to them? Just as in Deuteronomy, this is a matter of life and death, and far too many pastors who deeply believe that God does speak have abandoned His voice in Scripture.

Second, *God's true people are those who hear God speaking to them.* Time and time again in Deuteronomy, Moses says to the people, "Remember who you are! You are the people to whom Yahweh spoke, the people who received the Word of God at Horeb. He did not speak to everyone, only to you!" The point here is that the doctrine of revelation is directly tied to the doctrine of election. How do we know who God's people are? God's people are those to whom He speaks. The fact is, God did not speak to all the nations of the earth. He spoke to Israel, and by that they were identified as His chosen people.

By reminding the Israelites that God spoke to them alone, Moses was not trying to incite the Israelites to pride, arrogance, or self-confidence. On the contrary, he was telling them to humble themselves, realizing that it was only by grace and mercy that God chose to speak to Israel rather than to some other nation. "The LORD did not set His love on you nor choose you because you were more in number than any other people," he tells them in Deuteronomy 7:7, "for you were the least of all peoples." Rather, God chose to speak to them simply "because the LORD loves you, and because He would keep the oath which He swore to your fathers" (Deut. 7:8). Israel was indeed an elect, chosen, and blessed nation, but that status was all because of God's grace.

That is exactly the thrust of the passage in Deuteronomy 4:32–40, where Moses asks Israel four questions that are intended to remind them of how greatly and especially they have been blessed. The first of those questions is in verse 32: "Indeed, ask now concerning the former days which were before you, since the day that God created man on the earth, and inquire from one end of the heavens to the other. Has anything been done like this great thing?" (NASB). The exodus, the crushing of Pharaoh's army, the giving of the law, the entirety of God's dealings with Israel—had anything like this ever happened before? The answer, of course, is no. Israel's experience with God was utterly unique, and that is how they could know that they were God's people.

At the end of verse 32 is the second question: "Or has anything been heard like it?" Was there even a rumor out there of another people saying that their god rescued them from slavery, spoke to them, and chose them for his own glory? No! Once again, Israel was alone in that experience.

A third question appears in verse 34: "Or did God ever try to go and take for Himself a nation from the midst of another nation, by trials, by signs, by wonders, by war, by a mighty hand and an outstretched arm, and by great terrors, according to all that the LORD your God did for you in Egypt before your eyes?" Among the nations of the world, Israel was a captive people, a nation of slaves. Yet their captivity was also the means by which God would make Himself known to them. By rescuing them from Egypt—indeed, by taking them, as the text puts it—with His outstretched arm, the Lord showed both to the world and to the Israelites themselves that they were His chosen and special people.

The fourth question is found in verse 33 (NASB), and it is one of the sweetest and most powerful questions asked anywhere in Scripture: "Has any people heard the voice of God speaking from the midst of the fire, as you have heard it, and survived?" How does Israel know that they are God's people? How do they know that He has chosen them, and them alone? It is because God spoke to them out of the fire, and they lived to tell about it. No other people on earth heard the voice of God speak from the fire. Only Israel, the chosen people of God.

The same idea is found in the New Testament too. In Matthew 13:11, Jesus says to His disciples, "It has been given to you to know the mysteries of the kingdom of heaven, but to them it has not been given." That realization did not lead the disciples to arrogance. It was not "given" to them to understand because of any merit in them. The disciples were given the gift of understanding because, in His sovereign grace, God determined to glorify Himself in them. They could know they belonged to Jesus precisely because to them it had been "given to you to know the mysteries of the kingdom of heaven." As Jesus tells them later, "Blessed are your eyes for they see, and your ears for they hear; for assuredly, I say to you that many prophets and righteous men desired to see what you see, and did not see it, and to hear what you hear, and did not hear it" (Matt. 13:16–17).

How do you know that you are a believer in the Lord Jesus Christ? How do you explain that? Quite simply, it is because you have heard the word of God, and you have believed it savingly. Throughout the New Testament, God's elect are called out and redeemed by means of hearing the word of God. In John 5:24–25, for example, Jesus says, "Most assuredly, I say to you, he who hears My word and believes in Him who sent Me has everlasting life, and shall not come into judgment, but has passed from death into life. Most assuredly, I say to you, the hour is coming, and now is, when the dead will hear the voice of the Son of God; and those who hear will live." The focus in this passage is on the spiritually dead (Jesus will talk about the rising of the physically dead a few verses later), and what brings these spiritually dead people to life is hearing the voice of the Son of God. Indeed, it is only those who hear His word and believe who pass from death to life and do not come into judgment.

The book of Acts also emphasizes over and over that the Holy Spirit uses the hearing of God's Word to bring about saving faith. In Acts 2:37, it is only after the people hear Peter's sermon that they cry out, "Brethren, what shall we do?" Acts 13:48 records that "when the Gentiles *heard this*, they were glad and glorified the word of the Lord. And as many as had been appointed to eternal life believed" (emphasis added). And Acts 16:14 says that the Lord "opened [Lydia's] heart to *heed* the things *spoken* by Paul" (emphasis added).

Paul makes this point most explicitly in Romans 10:13–14, where he writes: "For 'whoever calls on the name of the LORD shall be saved.' How then shall they call on Him in whom they have not believed? And how shall they believe in Him of whom they have not heard? And how shall they hear without a preacher?"

God's elect people—those who hear His voice and believe in Jesus Christ—are called out primarily by the preaching of the Word. Therefore to replace the expository preaching of God's Word with anything else at all is to abandon the means God has determined to use to call His people to Himself. Do you want to see the elect called out and redeemed under your ministry? Do you want to see sinners come to faith? Then your task really could not be clearer, for "faith comes by hearing, and hearing by the word of God" (Rom. 10:17).

Third, *God's people depend for their very lives on hearing His word.* For the Israelites, hearing God's word and obeying it was a matter of life and death. "Therefore keep His statutes and His commandments," Moses told them, "that it may go well with you and with your children after you, and that you may prolong your days in the land which the LORD your God is giving you for all time" (Deut. 4:40). He makes the point again near the end of the book, in Deuteronomy 30:15–20:

> "See, I have set before you today life and good, death and evil, in that I command you today to love the LORD your God, to walk in His ways, and to keep His commandments, His statutes, and His judgments, that you may live and multiply; and the LORD your God will bless you in the land which you go to possess. But if your heart turns away so that you do not hear, and are drawn away, and worship other gods and serve them, I announce to you today that you shall surely perish; you shall not prolong your days in the land which you cross over the Jordan to go in and possess. I call heaven and earth as witnesses today against you, that I have set before you life and death, blessing and cursing; therefore choose life, that both you and your descendants may live; that you may love the LORD your God, that you may obey His voice, and that you may cling to Him, for He is your life and the length of your days; and

that you may dwell in the land which the LORD swore to your fathers, to Abraham, Isaac, and Jacob, to give them."

For Israel, God's word was like the manna in the wilderness. They needed it every day, fresh and new, if they were to survive at all. To hear the word and obey it was life for them. Not to hear and not to obey would result in death. So Israel lived by God's word, and that word became to them health, life, blessing, and even identity.

Read the Psalms, and you will see how Israel longed to hear and know God's word. King David says in Psalm 19, for example,

> The law of the LORD is perfect, converting the soul;
> The testimony of the LORD is sure, making wise the simple;
> The statutes of the LORD are right, rejoicing the heart;
> The commandment of the LORD is pure, enlightening the eyes;
> The fear of the LORD is clean, enduring forever;
> The judgments of the LORD are true and righteous altogether.
> More to be desired are they than gold,
> Yea, than much fine gold;
> Sweeter also than honey and the honeycomb.
> Moreover by them Your servant is warned,
> And in keeping them there is great reward....
> Let the words of my mouth and the meditation of my heart
> Be acceptable in Your sight,
> O LORD, my strength and my Redeemer. (vv. 7–11, 14)

Psalm 119 similarly declares the psalmist's dependence on the word of God:

> Unless Your law had been my delight,
> I would then have perished in my affliction.
> I will never forget Your precepts,
> For by them You have given me life.
> I am Yours, save me;
> For I have sought Your precepts.
> The wicked wait for me to destroy me,
> But I will consider Your testimonies. (vv. 92–95)

The people of Israel could not survive without the constant presence, knowledge, and hearing of God's word.

The same is true in the New Testament. Paul gives this eloquent testimony in 2 Timothy 3:16–17: "All Scripture is given by inspiration of God, and is profitable for doctrine, for reproof, for correction, for instruction in righteousness, that the man of God may be complete, thoroughly equipped for every good work." Scripture alone is breathed out by God, and thus it alone is profitable for these things. Nothing else in the world is. This is a testimony not only to the authority and perfection of Scripture but also to its sufficiency. It alone is sufficient for the teaching, reproof, correction, and training of God's people. As Christians, we live by the word of God just as completely as Israel did. We know who God is only through the Scriptures, and we know who we are in Christ only through the Scriptures.

Preaching is, therefore, always a matter of life and death. The people in our churches depend for their very lives on the ministry of the Word; therefore, our preaching had better be nothing less—and nothing other—than the exposition of the Bible. Nothing else will do. The question that faces us as preachers is not how we are going to grow our churches or inspire our people. It is not even how we can lead them to live more faithfully than they did before. The question that faces us is this: Are these people going to live, or are they going to die?

That is what was at stake in the Old Testament, and so it is also with Christian preaching. We have the Bible, and if we truly believe that Bible to be the written word of God—the perfect, divinely inspired revelation of God—then expositional preaching is the only option available to us.

It all finally comes down to the question of who has the right to speak. Does the preacher have the right to speak, or does that right belong to God? That is the difference between life and death for our people. Do we think that God's elect will be called out by our own stories, gimmicks, and eloquence? Such thinking is arrogance. Can God's redeemed people live on our words alone? Will they be just fine if we don't read and explain God's Word to them? Obviously not, for life is found only in the Word of God.

In the end, our calling as preachers is really very simple. We study, we stand before our people, we read the text, and we explain it. We reprove, rebuke, exhort, encourage, and teach—and then we do it all again and again and again.

CHAPTER 6

Preaching as Transformation

Derek W. H. Thomas

> *And [Jesus] preached the word to them.*
> —Mark 2:2

The goal of redemption is Jesus-likeness: "For whom He foreknew, He also predestined to be conformed to the image of His Son" (Rom. 8:29). God saves sinners by giving them a new heart and then eventually sanctifying them "completely" (1 Thess. 5:23). Regeneration and progressive sanctification are divinely designed to bring about total moral and spiritual transformation. This, in its details and eventual accomplishment, is a work of the Holy Spirit—monergistically in our regeneration and the definitive aspect of our sanctification (see John 3:3, 5; 1 Cor. 1:2), but cooperatively and synergistically in the lifelong, progressive aspect of our sanctification. In the latter case we "work out [our] salvation with fear and trembling," responding to the invitations, threats, and promises, knowing that God is at work in us (Phil. 2:12–13).

How is this goal of eventual Christlikeness to be achieved in a post-Christian, secular world? The answer is the same for us as it was for those in the first century: spiritual and moral transformation is achieved through the "foolishness of the message preached" (1 Cor. 1:21). The primacy given to the role of preaching in Scripture is designed to address all cultures in all ages and circumstances. While personal mentorship, group activities, Bible studies, and prayer fellowships play vital roles, it is the activity of preaching—Bible exposition and application delivered in the form of a sermon—that God has ordained as the means to accomplish the task of conforming His redeemed children to be like His Son.

And what is preaching, precisely? Outside of a commitment to Scripture's absolute authority, there are multiple answers to this question. Assuming a commitment to the Bible's inerrant quality, a *biblical* definition of preaching must include some key features. Though preaching does have an institutional dimension (it involves pulpits or platforms, pews or padded chairs) as well as a sociological dimension (it is something that happens in a group setting), theologically, preaching is a God-ordained, Bible-based activity of exposition and application typically delivered through a Spirit-gifted person according to interpretive rules that complement the Bible's view of itself as totally trustworthy and reliable in such a way that what the Bible says, God says.

Healthy Christians and healthy churches are utterly dependent on biblical preaching. Without it, Christians and churches drift into sacramentalism (an exaggerated belief in the power of sacred ritual) or nominalism (a diminished belief that no religious ceremony is of any great value). In churches where preaching is central and of paramount importance, church architecture has reflected this with central pulpits and building design that maximizes the spoken (and heard) Word. The cultural shift to nearly invisible pulpits and platforms that enable preachers to walk from side to side often comes with questionable emphasis upon the preacher rather than the Word of God. Skinny jeans and visible tattoos may demonstrate (sadly) a sexy authenticity, but they do nothing to ensure the centrality of the Word of God. I make the point not out of a mere sentiment for tradition but out of a concern for the ever-decreasing centrality of Scripture in much current worship.

To elaborate, not all that bears the name "preaching" *is* preaching. Discourses, of whatever length and content, that fail to open up and apply the meaning of the text of Scripture are, frankly, something else—speeches, orations, pep talks, rallies, motivational addresses, diatribes—call them what you will. J. I. Packer writes on the topic, thus:

> Sermons (Latin, *sermons*, speeches) are often composed and delivered on wrong principles. Thus, if they fail to open Scripture or they expound it without applying it, or if they are no more than lectures aimed at informing the mind or addresses seeking only to focus the present self-awareness of the listening group, or if they are delivered as statements of the preacher's opinion rather than as messages from God, or if their lines of thought do not require listeners to change in any way, they fall short of being preaching, just as they would if they were so random and confused that no one could tell what the speaker was saying. It is often said, and truly, that sermons must teach, and the current level of knowledge (ignorance, rather) in the Christian world is such that the need for sermons that teach cannot be questioned for one moment. But preaching is essentially teaching *plus* application (invitation, direction,

summons); where the *plus* is lacking, something less than preaching occurs. And many in the church have never experienced preaching in this full biblical sense of the word.[1]

The "So What" Factor

Preaching is teaching *plus* application. To suggest that preaching is application is to overstate the case, but unless there is a "so what?" component, it is something less than preaching.[2] This has to be said in the face of some intense opinion to the contrary. The view of preaching that suggests that all application is legalism—indicative as this is of a growing culture of antinomianism—is one such example. Another, and perhaps related to it, is an extreme form of redemptive-historical preaching that studiously disdains all application other than a "Let's see Jesus or the gospel" in this text.[3] My desire is not to deprecate the idea of a redemptive-historical hermeneutic. On the contrary—I regard this as an essential step in the discernment of the biblical text's meaning. Without it, the road leads to moralism. My concern is a view that insists that this is all there is to the meaning of the text; everything becomes a statement about justification by faith alone apart from works, and all imperatives are viewed suspiciously as backdoor attempts to undermine the gospel. Such preaching destroys application at its root and, frankly, seems alien to examples of preaching in the New Testament.

The subject before us, then, in this chapter could hardly be more important: How does preaching bring about transformation in the lives of God's children? Vital issues are in play. True preaching—*biblical* preaching—involves both *explanation* and *application, indicative* and *imperative, proclamation* and *appeal.*[4] At the heart of the issue lie basic tensions between law and gospel, and, as Luther expressed it, "Whoever knows well how to distinguish the Gospel from the Law should give thanks to God and know that

---

1. J. I. Packer, "Why Preach?," in *Honouring the Written Word of God*, vol. 3 of *Collected Shorter Writings* (Carlisle, Pa.: Paternoster Press, 1999), 248. Also published as the introduction to *The Preacher and Preaching*, ed. Samuel T. Logan (Phillipsburg, N.J.: Presbyterian and Reformed, 1986), 1–29.

2. See John F. Bettler, "Application," in *Preacher and Preaching*, 332, 344.

3. For a masterful critique of the redemptive-historical hermeneutic from one who is totally sympathetic to its main goals, see Richard B. Gaffin, *Redemptive History and Biblical Interpretation: The Shorter Writings of Geerhardus Vos*, ed. Richard B. Gaffin Jr. (Phillipsburg, N.J.: Presbyterian and Reformed, 1980).

4. See John Carrick, *The Imperative of Preaching: A Theology of Sacred Rhetoric* (Edinburgh: Banner of Truth, 1982), 82–146.

he is a real theologian."[5] It is no exaggeration, therefore, to view the function
and manner of application in preaching as reflective of our understanding
of the nature of the Christian life—what we *are* in Christ and what we are *to
become* in Christ. To rest in the indicatives is to miss the apostolic concern
for vigorous and detailed repentance and conformity to Christlikeness that
ongoing sanctification (progressive as well as positional) requires.

The Holy Spirit attends the reading of Scripture, but the Spirit makes
preaching "an effectual means of enlightening, convincing and humbling
sinners."[6] Preaching, attended by the power and blessing of the Holy Spirit,
is God's primary means of applying the benefits of all that Christ has accomplished. By it, sinners are called, quickened, justified, sanctified, and glorified
(see Rom. 8:29–30). So closely related is the advance and growth of the church
(numerically and spiritually) that Luke employs a synecdoche—"the word of
God grew and multiplied" (Acts 12:24). It is Christians who multiplied, in
number and godliness, but so attached was this to the preaching of Scripture
that the apostle describes the circumstance as the increase of Scripture itself!
And he never lost sight of this powerful use of Scripture, urging in his final
epistle to his brother and successor Timothy: "Preach the word! Be ready in
season and out of season. Convince, rebuke, exhort, with all longsuffering
and teaching" (2 Tim. 4:2).

Experiential Preaching

Preaching, yes! But what kind of preaching? And, more specifically, to what
end? A term employed to describe preaching that includes a specific kind
of application is experiential preaching.[7] Writing in 1835, Robert Burns
described experiential preaching this way:

---

5. In *Galatians 1–4*, vol. 26 of *Luther's Works* (St. Louis: Concordia, 1968), 115.
6. Westminster Larger Catechism 159. For a helpful summary of the teaching of the
sixteenth-century Reformed confessions on preaching, see Cornelis Venema, "The Doctrine
of Preaching in the Reformed Confessions," *Mid-America Journal of Theology* 10 (1999):
135–83; and A. D. Strange, "Comments on the Centrality of Preaching in the Westminster
Standards," *Mid-America Journal of Theology* 10 (1999): 185–238.
7. The contemporary Christian philosopher Paul Helm prefers to employ the term
"experimental preaching": "'Experimental' preaching means preaching that is testing,
preaching that directs the believer to self-examination and action, not preaching that is dry
or academic in tone or content. Nor preaching that is 'experiential' (in some generalized
sense). Such preaching ought not to be some exotic, occasional exercise, but rather part of
the staple diet of the Christian church, by which the wheat is separated from the chaff, and
the believer is established in the faith that works by love." Paul Helm, "'Experimental' or

Christianity brought home to men's business and bosoms.... The principle on which experimental religion rests is simply this, that Christianity should not only be known, and understood, and believed, but also felt, and enjoyed, and practically applied.[8]

Assuming Aristotle was correct in suggesting that the first consideration ought to be the final goal one wishes to achieve, a great deal of preaching fails precisely for this reason. Lacking a goal, the sermon never lands anywhere in particular. There is a vagueness as to the point of the sermon. There is information, yes. Mercifully, there is evidence of exegesis. There appears to be evidence that commentaries have been consulted. Convinced that there is meaning in the text, the sermon has something to say, something of great import and relevance. There is often enthusiasm and emotion. But there is little if any conviction, a disturbance of the soul that evokes a sense of urgency and self-denying commitment. Nor, sadly, does the sermon ask of us any practical response other than to react in awe at the greatness of what God has done for us in the gospel. Surely there is more to preaching than this!

But we should pause and reflect on what has just been said. Truth is a form of application. It is application to the mind, to the way we think. Folk require epistemological reshaping. People do dumb things because they are ignorant, sometimes willfully so. As John Stott marvelously expressed it in the title of his book first published in 1973, your mind matters.[9] I vividly recall reading this book when I was a freshman, newly converted to Christ. I can still recall the force of the metaphor employed from Psalm 32:9 and to which Stott referred—don't be like a horse or mule that needs prodding into activity—but *use your mind*. There is a mindless form of Christianity that may not even be Christianity at all, but something entirely different.

Stott's point was to address the false dichotomy between Christian truth and Christian experience. Evangelical Christianity in the mid-twentieth century (at least in Britain, his principal audience) had become wary of intellectual approaches to Christianity. Consequently, doctrine and what we would now call apologetic approaches were beginning to be shunned. Stott's

---

'Experiential'?," *Helm's Deep* (blog), October 1, 2013, http://www.paulhelmsdeep.blogspot.com/2013_10_01_archive.html.

8. Robert Burns, introductory essay to *The Works of Thomas Halyburton* (London: Thomas Tegg and Son, 1835), xiv–xv.

9. John Stott, *Your Mind Matters: The Place of the Mind in the Christian Life* (1973; repr., Downers Grove, Ill.: InterVarsity, 2006).

concern was that evangelicals were failing to answer the questions raised by
post-Enlightenment liberalism, huddling into a ghetto mentality and avoiding the call of Christianity to engage the academy. Stott called for a robust
intellectual approach to evangelicalism that avoided checking one's mind at
the door of the church only to pick it up again on the way out. Christianity
is first an exposition of what is true, what every Christian needs to believe.
Christianity must be intellectually rigorous if it is to meet the challenge of
unbelief. It is what Paul seemed most concerned with—"sound doctrine" and
"good doctrine" (1 Tim. 1:10; 4:6; Titus 1:9; 2:1), in contrast with "every wind
of doctrine" (Eph. 4:14).

Truth matters, and, in a sense, it is application. For this reason, it is often
misleading to divide sermons into exposition followed by application, suggesting that exposition plays no part in changing how Christians respond to
what they hear. Understanding the truth—epistemological rigor—is essential if we are to understand who God is and what He has done and what He
expects of us in return. It is particularly galling—a practice that needs to
be stopped immediately—when preachers say, often because time is running
short, "I need to make a few quick points of application now," suggesting as
they do so that everything that has occurred up until this point has been
something entirely different—of no practical value at all. Let's call an immediate moratorium on this silly practice.

Preaching as Grammatical-Historical Exposition of Words

Grammatical-historical preaching is a method that seeks to uncover the
original author's intended meaning as contained in the analysis of words
and their meaning individually and collectively in sentences, paragraphs,
and books and in the original setting in which they were first delivered. This
view of preaching, which underlines the importance of the spoken and written word, reflects the way in which God communicates to us. He spoke the
universe into being. His Son and our Mediator is the Word (*Logos*) of God.
All that we need to know concerning truth and life is set down in written
form—in words, sentences, verbs, pronouns, and grammatical rules. Preaching is making God's will known through expounding the meaning of what is
written in Scripture. The only right a preacher has to demand that he be listened to is the authority of Scripture as God's inerrant word. True, that word
is presented incarnationally—in words given expression and life through a
particular individual (think again of Phillips Brooks's oft-cited definition of

preaching, "truth through personality")—but everything that is said is based on the authority of the written Word of God, rightly understood and applied.

Preaching, then, is first of all the communication of truth, ideas, worldviews, and mind-shaping analyses of what is wrong with the world and how God has proposed and ensured its redemption through faith in Jesus Christ. Its purpose is to inform and persuade, not by circumventing the intellect and reason but by engaging both.

How Can We Then Live?

But preaching must also be applicatory. How can it not be? Its purpose is to reshape us and the cosmos in which we live. It is concerned with the great question posed in Ezekiel 33:10: "How can we then live?" Truth in itself, even if presented with great passion and energy, requires something more to fully become what we term preaching. It requires exhortation, warning, urging, declamation, wooing, and enticing to effectively change us in some spiritual or practical way. As Paul put it in Romans 12, a combination of "body" and "mind": "I beseech you therefore, brethren, by the mercies of God, that you present your bodies a living sacrifice, holy, acceptable to God, which is your reasonable service. And do not be conformed to this world, but be transformed by the renewing of your mind, that you may prove what is that good and acceptable and perfect will of God" (Rom. 12:1–2).

Reflecting on a lifetime of preaching, Alec Motyer writes, "What we need in our pulpits is didactic and applicatory exposition."[10] Carefully explaining exposition as "drawing out from the Word of God what the Holy Spirit has deposited there without addition, subtraction or modification," Motyer then delineates its twin components, "truth to be grasped" and "truth to be believed." Defining the latter, he has this to say: "'Applicatory': the Word of God brought home to the hearers as truth to be believed, a way of life to be followed, a rule to be obeyed, a promise to be embraced, a sin to be avoided, an example to be followed and a blessing to be enjoyed."[11]

None of this is new. In the early seventeenth century, William Perkins, in a commentary on Galatians, wrote in similar fashion on "effectual and powerful preaching of the Word":

---

10. Alec Motyer, *Preaching? Simple Teaching on Simply Preaching* (Fearn, Ross-shire, Scotland: Christian Focus, 2013), 101.

11. Motyer, *Preaching? Simple Teaching*, 103.

The first is true and proper interpretation of the Scripture, and that by itself. For Scripture is both the gloss [or interpretation, explanation] and the text. The second is savory and wholesome doctrine, gathered out of the Scriptures truly expounded. The third is the application of the said doctrine, either to the information of the judgment or to the reformation of the life. This is the preaching that is of power. Let all the sons of the prophets think upon these things, and study to be doers of them.[12]

Perkins engaged in what we might call today "audience analysis." Distinguishing different groups in his audience, Perkins perceived that a corresponding difference in application is required—the same truth applied in different ways to different individuals or groups. These categories include the following: ignorant and unreachable unbelievers; ignorant but teachable; knowledgeable but not humbled; the humbled—either partly or thoroughly; those who are already believers; backsliders of various kinds; congregations containing a mixture of believers and unbelievers.[13]

These are broad categories that could easily be refined and expanded. The point of the division is to alert the discerning preacher to what different groups of people need to hear. For example, young believers whose inward and outward fires are burning brightly can easily be discouraged. They can easily be led into activity without knowing the reason for it. Older Christians, passing through the spiritual equivalent of a midlife crisis, are tempted into cynicism by trial and failure. They have different issues to face. Unlike young believers, they are tempted to give up. And Christians at the end of their pilgrimage, looking forward to an eternal rest and finding the wait long and difficult, require a more gentle application. They desire to persevere but lack the strength to accomplish it. They fear that their light will expire before they reach the end of their journey.

What Perkins is warning us against is a "one-size-fits-all" approach to application, the desperate attempt of a preacher who has spent too long in exposition and now, needing something to say by way of application, blurts out the first thing that comes into his head, irrelevant and misdirected as it so often can be. This does no justice to preaching and ultimately fails in its goal of shaping lives into Jesus-like conformity.

---

12. *Commentary on Galatians*, vol. 2 of *The Works of William Perkins*, ed. Paul M. Smalley (Grand Rapids: Reformation Heritage Books, 2015), 148 (commenting on Gal. 3:1).

13. In early Puritan England, nonattendance at worship on the Sabbath was liable to a fine; therefore, the presence of unbelievers in public worship services needed to be addressed.

Bringing the Text Home

A few decades after Perkins, sixteenth-century preacher-theologians contin- ued to think through the task of preaching and the role of application. In what continues to be an outstanding summary of the essential aspects of biblical preaching, the Westminster divines insisted that preaching should include "raising doctrines from the text," adding, by way of exhortation to preachers,

> He is not to rest in general doctrine, although never so much cleared and confirmed, but to bring it home to special use, by application to his hearers: which albeit it prove a work of great difficulty to himself, requiring much prudence, zeal, and meditation, and to the natural and corrupt man will be very unpleasant; yet he is to endeavour to perform it in such a manner, that his auditors may feel the word of God to be quick and powerful, and a discerner of the thoughts and intents of the heart; and that, if any unbeliever or ignorant person be present, he may have the secrets of his heart made manifest, and give glory to God.[14]

So essential is application to preaching that without it, we are left with some- thing other than a sermon. "Doctrine is but the drawing of the bow," wrote the Puritan Thomas Manton; "application is hitting the mark."[15]

These theologians based their ideas about preaching and application on Paul's statement regarding the use of Scripture in his swan-song epistle, 2 Timothy. Following the apostle's declaration of the nature of Scripture as God-breathed (3:16, *theopneustos*), he elaborates on the fourfold use of Scripture: "All Scripture is given by inspiration of God, and is profitable for doctrine, for reproof, for correction, for instruction in righteousness, that the man of God may be complete, thoroughly equipped for every good work" (2 Tim. 3:16–17).

Blessed Are the Persecuted

To see how this fourfold use of Scripture applies to preaching, consider, by way of a single example, a well-known text of Scripture from the Sermon on the Mount—the eighth and final beatitude: "Blessed are those who are per- secuted for righteousness' sake, for theirs is the kingdom of heaven. Blessed

---

14. The Directory for the Publick Worship of God, in *Westminster Confession of Faith* (1645; repr., Glasgow: Free Presbyterian Publications, 1970), 380.

15. Thomas Manton, *A Practical Commentary, or an Exposition, with Notes, on the Epis- tle of James* (London: James Nisbet, 1871), 357.

are you when they revile and persecute you, and say all kinds of evil against you falsely for My sake. Rejoice and be exceedingly glad, for great is your reward in heaven, for so they persecuted the prophets who were before you" (Matt. 5:10–12).

Consider, also, just one truth taught in this beatitude (and there are several)—that suffering lies at the heart of true Christian discipleship. Not just suffering in the abstract or suffering caused by selfish and willful behavior on our part, but suffering that is the result of opposition to Christlikeness. What life-altering application should we make to the various groups who may be listening to our sermon?

The unconverted may not want to think that coming to faith in Christ may cost them physical harm. Like the rich young ruler, perhaps, they are not prepared for the cost and walk away. Perhaps the application is to note that this is exactly what they are doing. "You do not want a relationship that may injure your precarious self-esteem, and therefore you are saying no to this path. And because you are saying no, Jesus is saying no to you."

What about those who are inquiring, wondering what Christianity is all about? Do they need to be reprimanded or enticed? Are they genuinely asking what following Jesus will be like? What if they have moved on? They are "not far from the kingdom of God" (Mark 12:34). They can glimpse the kingdom but are unsure that they will have the will or strength to meet its challenges. The preacher must encourage them to persevere in their path toward grasping the Savior in the knowledge that at every stage, Jesus will supply what He demands.

What about the newly converted? They are ready to die for Jesus. Their relationship with the Lord is so intense that they are in danger of encouraging persecution through lack of wisdom. They have a zeal, but "not according to knowledge" (Rom. 10:2). Maybe what this category of persons needs is some instruction on discernment, an understanding of what is primary and secondary, of what is biblical and what is prejudicial and legalistic. Perhaps, too, there is a danger of pride that comes with such zeal and the subsequent fall that so often follows: "Pride goes before destruction, and a haughty spirit before a fall" (Prov. 16:18).

And what of those who find themselves at the end of their journey? Can they expect discouragement and opposition? Has not the length of their discipleship proved sufficient to resist all forms of persecution? Perhaps the application will need to come in ensuring a form of perseverance "to the end"—"he who endures to the end shall be saved" (Matt. 10:22; 24:13; cf.

Heb. 3:14). Perhaps, too, they may need the added encouragement of a promise that the Lord will sustain them "to the end" (1 Cor. 1:8).

And what of those who find themselves in trouble—manifestly so because they have fallen into trouble of their own making? They have sinned, privately or publicly, and are reaping the distress and dislocation that ensues from such behavior. Perhaps they are excusing themselves and complaining about their trouble. They need the reprimand of God's word. They are like the one envisaged in Proverbs who is caught in "calamity" (1:26) because they have refused to listen to words of wisdom (1:24–25).

And what of those who have fallen through no fault of their own—the Job-like pilgrims who now walk in distress and trouble, who might even find themselves in the darkest of places, regretting ("cursing") their birth and existence (Job 3; Jer. 20:7–18)? They are not remotely near rejoicing in their tribulation (Rom. 5:3–5). What application must be given to them? Should it be a word of instruction about so-called innocent suffering that addresses their understanding? Should they should hear a word of encouragement that motivates them to a better place, for continuing in this state is only going to make things worse for them and everyone around them? Perhaps, but we might imagine they already know this and feel powerless to do anything about it. Perhaps it is a word of encouragement that they need—that they are not alone, despite feeling desperately so. Our Savior has walked this path, one in which He seemed to lose all sense of His native Sonship and could only cry, "My God, My God, why have You forsaken Me?" (Matt. 27:46; Mark 15:34).

Too many preachers also leave application to the end of the sermon. It is doubtful if this practice ever accomplishes a great deal. Truth needs to be applied as soon as it is made clear, and, therefore, applications ought to pepper the entire sermon.

Too many preachers leave the application of a sermon to take care of itself. Having given attention to the introduction and structure of the sermon, they give too little thought to the target of the sermon. For some, as we mentioned earlier, all application of the kind mentioned in our example above borders (and perhaps transgresses) upon a perceived legalism. The point of the sermon is Christ, and not our doing. A sermon that ends with a series of imperatives seems to violate the gospel. It becomes an instruction manual in doing when the gospel is telling us that it is done. These are false dichotomies that fail the most basic test—that the New Testament itself is full of directives and commands for Christians to heed and follow.

Archibald Alexander, the first professor of Princeton Theological Seminary, was convinced that many sermons failed to make adequate distinctions among the recipients. The application was too vague and too randomly addressed: "How often do we hear a preacher expatiating on the rich consolations of the exceeding great and precious promises of God, when no mortal can tell, from anything which he says, to whom they are applicable. In much preaching, there is a vague and indiscriminate application of the special promises of the Covenant of Grace, as though all who had heard them are true Christians, and had a claim to the comfort which they offer." And again: "So preach the Gospel that impenitent sinners may not only be convinced that they are in a lost condition; but that their course is unreasonable, and that the whole blame of their destruction will be at their own door.[16] James Garretson, from whose book on Archibald Alexander the quotation above is taken, adds some comments of his own that are helpful here. "True biblical preaching," he writes, "will draw a clear line of distinction between the saint and the sinner; people will not be confused about their true spiritual state."[17]

Conclusion

What have we said in this chapter? In brief compass, this:

- Preaching is the chief means God employs in birthing and growing His church.
- Preaching is itself concerned with expounding Scripture—the whole Scripture and nothing but the Scripture.
- Preaching consists of explanation and application—both are equally necessary.
- Preaching effects change—spiritual and moral transformation—that involves the mind, the will, and the affections.
- Preaching requires sensitivity—to the text and what it is (and is not) saying; to the audience and the condition in which they find themselves.

There is a rich heritage of biblical preaching that exemplifies all of these characteristics, and my friend Dr. Steven J. Lawson exemplifies this tradition.

---

16. As quoted in James Garretson, *Princeton and Preaching: Archibald Alexander and the Christian Ministry* (Edinburgh: Banner of Truth, 2005), 168.

17. Garretson, *Princeton and Preaching*, 168.

The Reformation grew out of a rediscovery of the power of biblical preaching. The oft-maligned Puritan movement on both sides of the Atlantic displayed a robust commitment to such preaching. The Great Awakening in New England and the accompanying awakenings in the eighteenth century reflected a belief in the power of biblical preaching that effected the transformation of individuals and communities beyond recognition. Nineteenth-century preachers like Charles Haddon Spurgeon and twentieth-century preachers like Donald Barnhouse and Martyn Lloyd-Jones continued this testimony to the power of biblical preaching.

As a seminary professor for two decades, I see some encouraging signs of what may lie ahead for us as a church. In my own small corner alone, I witness on an annual basis dozens of gifted men train as preachers and embark on a mission in which preaching is central to their calling. Quibbles apart about this or that aspect of their preaching, I see an army of seminary-trained expositors give their lives to a task the world considers hopeless and misguided. I hear their unwavering commitment to the inerrancy of Scripture and a belief that Scripture properly taught and applied can transform lives and communities. In the culture of despair and retreat that so often characterizes our modern church, there are signs of immense optimism.

True, there are skeptics—in the pulpit and in the pew. Arrogant young men with too much trust in their own importance eventually fall—and bring disgrace on themselves and those around them. And small-minded worshipers who flatten expectation, thinking that nothing much is going to happen in the sermon, consequently sit back and wait impatiently for the service to end when real things happen. Yes, these things are true. And it underlines that it takes "two to tango," as they say, and expectant listeners must combine with committed preachers if true preaching and consequent transformation is going to take place.

Expectant listeners and faithful preachers—these are what we need most in our time. And in my friend Steve Lawson, we have an example of a faithful preacher committed to the twin tasks of rightly dividing the Word of God and providing close application. The Lord enable those of us who are preachers to follow his example and all of us who are listeners to be grateful that every gospel-based imperative is designed to make us more like the Lord Jesus.

CHAPTER 7

Preaching as Worship

Sinclair B. Ferguson

Here is a scenario that probably many guest preachers have experienced, somewhat to their surprise: Someone other than the "lead pastor"—a young associate pastor or someone introducing himself as the "worship leader"— welcomes those who have gathered. He says something like this: "A warm welcome to everyone today! For the first half hour we will have a time of worship, and then Pastor Ricky will teach us from the Bible. Then we'd like to meet you over coffee in the lounge."

Something isn't quite right here. It certainly isn't the warmth of the welcome. It isn't the little indication of a fear of the old-fashioned title "senior pastor/minister" and the use of the substitute "lead pastor," with its curiously counterintentionally greater emphasis on the individual's role as "first." Even his misguided self-description as the "worship leader" can be overlooked because we know what he means. That said, he will be embarrassed if you gently tell him that actually the Lord Jesus Christ is the worship leader of His gathered people.[1] It isn't the desire to help visitors and outsiders have some idea of what to expect. Nor is it even that anything approaching a classical invitation to "Let us worship God" is missing. Not even his reference to the preacher as Pastor Ricky phases you.

No, what most deeply concerns you is that he has separated worship from preaching—perhaps even without realizing he is doing it or the implications of doing so. He probably does not know that in the best days of the church's existence the reading and preaching of the Scriptures not only shaped worship but were seen as the heart of worship itself. For then God speaks through

---

1. That Christ is our worship leader is a theological point of considerable significance because it expresses a view of worship quite different from the current "worship-leader" phenomenon.

His word, from His heart to His people's hearts, as surely as if His voice is heard.[2] Thus, the deepest sense of worship is intended to take place during and because of the preaching. It is in this way that the most interior soul engagement with the Lord is ordinarily to be experienced and the profoundest responses of praise evoked.

Paul gives us a hint of this in the context of the apparent free-for-all that was marring worship among the spiritually multigifted Corinthians. "Be more discerning," he pleads; "in your thinking be mature. If a stranger comes into the service and finds everyone speaking in tongues with none to interpret, he will question the congregation's sanity. But if someone is prophesying"—which, in this context, means expounding divine revelation—"then the stranger will be convicted and called to account. The secrets of his heart are disclosed, and, so, falling on his face, he will worship God and declare that He is really among you." This is the heart of our experience of worship:

> God Himself is with us;
> Let us now adore Him,
> And with awe appear before Him.[3]

If this is true of the unbeliever, how much more will it be true of believers? When this happens it will become clear why the Westminster Larger Catechism teaches this lesson about preaching:

Q. 155: How is the word of God made effectual to salvation?

A. The Spirit of God maketh the reading, but especially the preaching of the word, an effectual means of enlightening, convincing, and humbling sinners; of driving them out of themselves, and drawing them unto Christ.

This is what happens in true worship.

It was the preaching of cherubim on the holiness of God that led Isaiah to the deepest worship experience he had ever known (Isa. 6:1–3). Nor should we miss the point that their own worship was expressed in that preaching and that their preaching was also an expression of their worship. No matter

---

2. Calvin famously speaks about regarding the Scriptures as "having sprung from heaven, as if there the living words of God were heard." John Calvin, *Institutes of the Christian Religion*, trans. Ford Lewis Battles, ed. John T. McNeill (Philadelphia: Westminster Press, 1960), 1.7.1.

3. Gerhardt Tersteegen, "God Himself Is with Us," public domain.

how often Isaiah had been at services in the Jerusalem temple, that day he must have felt as though he had "gone to worship" for the first time in his life!

Worship and preaching, therefore, belong together. Through the ministry of the Spirit, preaching is worship and also evokes worship. The question we therefore need to explore is this: What kind of preaching most expresses and evokes worship?

While there is no extended discussion of this theme in the New Testament, it is punctuated with clues that help us to answer the question. Some of the most important are found in Paul's last letter to his evangelist-disciple Timothy. Having enunciated the divine origin that Timothy has long trusted, he focuses in particular on the Scripture's usefulness and how this is related to the preaching of the Word.

The Scriptures are useful for teaching (revelation enlightening the mind); for reproving (reaching into and convicting the conscience); for correcting (Paul's word *epanorthōsis* carries the sense of restoration and draws attention to a much-neglected element in biblical teaching and, consequently, for preaching); and for training in righteousness (*paideia*, spiritual child-rearing) (2 Tim. 3:16).

It is, however, what Paul goes on to say that underlines the significance of these words not merely for Timothy's preaching: since these are the qualities of Scripture, he is to preach it in these terms, using God's word to reprove, rebuke, and teach and to do so with patience and perseverance (2 Tim. 4:2). So must we.

The chapter break in 2 Timothy between chapters 3 and 4 too often obscures the connection Paul makes between the origin and usefulness of the word and preaching. In essence he seems to be saying, "If Scripture is God-breathed (*theopneustos*) in order to be useful in these ways, then preach it accordingly." He thus provides us with a fourfold preaching grid of teaching, reproving, correcting, and child-training. When preaching exhibits these characteristics, worship follows: God's people recognize His voice; He speaks in holy love, and at least inwardly we fall down and say, "God is here." The preaching of the Word becomes a Jacob's ladder into the presence of God. As hearers we are "lost in wonder, love and praise."[4]

The evidences of this? People respond variously, saying, "What God is teaching us is clearer to me now. I never saw it before." "I sensed my sin and need exposed." "Although I was so deeply convicted, I feel wonderfully

---

4. Charles Wesley, "Love Divine, All Loves Excelling," public domain.

comforted and encouraged." "The Lord brought pardon and peace and hope and assurance to me." "I feel better equipped to serve the Savior, and by His grace I will." This is the intended effect of preaching in which teaching, reproof, correction, and child-training take place. The result? The singing of the psalm, hymn, or spiritual song that follows the preaching is climactic—more whole-souled than any praise that preceded it. When "the voice of the LORD" that is "powerful" and "full of majesty" is heard, "in His temple everyone says, 'Glory!'" (Ps. 29:4, 9). Then we "worship the LORD in the beauty of holiness" (Ps. 29:2).

If worship is the goal of preaching, then as preachers we must have this apostolic grid in mind as we prepare, as we preach, as we look for fruit, and as we assess our own preaching.[5] It is not the only preaching grid found in Scripture, but it has both a simplicity and an obvious applicability that makes it particularly significant in the nurturing and nourishing of a worshiping people. It is also a valuable litmus test and can also act as a catalyst to recalibrate and rebalance our preaching according to Scripture.

This is important because not all preaching equally expresses the worship of the preacher or creates a worshipful people. Imbalance in the four elements Paul mentions to Timothy produces imbalance in our people. Thus, to take one example, preaching dominated by doctrinal instruction ("teaching") but lacking in "correction" (in the positive sense above) may leave us well informed but undernourished. Again, preaching that aims at "reproof" or "conviction" (of sin) without "teaching" on how the gospel brings forgiveness and restoration and also enables transition to greater conformity to Christ leaves us conscious that we are not like Christ, but without the hope of grace that worship always involves.

In contrast, God seeks the worship of people who are being renewed in every aspect of their being. Sanctification through the truth, which is the word of God, is not purely cerebral any more than it is largely negative or emotional. But where all the elements of this apostolic grid are present, then, through the Spirit's ministry, true worship will be the result.

---

5. Its fruitfulness lies in the hands of the Spirit, but its faithfulness to the content, the spirit, and the function of Scripture is our responsibility. If the Spirit is the ultimate soul surgeon, we are operating-room assistants and have an important responsibility to make sure we hand the Spirit Surgeon clean instruments for His spiritual surgery. He of course may act "without, above, and against" secondary means, but He characteristically makes use of pure vessels. Westminster Confession of Faith 5.4. Cf. 2 Timothy 2:20–26.

This is enormously challenging. One of the mysteries of preaching is that as the preacher's mental capacities are enlarged while he is preaching, his weaknesses and spiritual imbalances can be magnified as well. At the least they will be put on display. The distortion that results here will be imprinted, at times quite unconsciously, on the hearer. For believers are predisposed to hear the word of God through their ministers and to trust it. In doing so they tend to breathe in the proportionality and the atmospherics in which it is communicated. They come to associate the way we preach the Word to them with the word itself coming to them. They may not be employing the "Pauline assessment grid" and find discernment difficult. No wonder not many of us should be teachers, and no wonder that we should be judged by high standards—because the word that comes from our lips shapes the degree, manner, and affections of the worship of our congregation.

What will help us here as preachers? Ultimately that question can be answered only by whole volumes on preaching and by a whole lifetime of experience. But within the parameters of this essay, two foci are worth mentioning and reflecting on: (1) Christ's role in preaching and worship, (2) and the implications of this for the preacher and his preaching.

Christ and Our Preaching

It should go without saying to most readers that we are called to "preach Christ crucified" (1 Cor. 1:23), to be determined to "know nothing" among our congregation other than "Jesus Christ and Him crucified" (1 Cor. 2:2). It is one thing to declare this as our intention in our first sermon to a new congregation, and another to be able to preach on these texts with integrity at the end of our ministry. "Christ crucified" needs to be central in our message. Through Him we have access to the Father; from Him we receive the Holy Spirit (Eph. 2:18).

But there is another vital dimension characteristic of preaching that is both the worship of the preacher and evokes worship in the hearers: the Lord Jesus is not merely the subject of our preaching but He is Himself the preacher of our preaching. If I may interject a personal note here, the dawning of this reality shortly after my ordination to the gospel ministry has been, in a secondary sense, my salvation as a preacher. It is a key that has explained much and has also brought stability in days of failure and conflict as well as in days of harvest. Preacher and hearer alike sit under the preaching of Jesus in His Word. That is what brings both to worship.

First, the biblical evidence: This is, at least potentially, a transforming affirmation—that Christ Himself would be the preacher. But is it biblically rooted, or simply fanciful? Let us begin with Jesus's own teaching. Jesus, the good Shepherd, taught that He had "other sheep...which are not of this fold [i.e., His own Jewish people]; them also I must bring" (John 10:16). International members of the church are in view. He Himself will bring them into the fold. This "bringing" by Jesus takes place through the ministry of the *allos paraklētos*, the Holy Spirit, whom He has already promised (John 7:37–39).[6] "They will hear My voice" (John 10:16). Recognizing the voice of the Shepherd, His sheep follow Him (John 10:3–5). But where is the voice of Christ to be heard?

In Johannine terms the answer is in the words of the apostles. They are being prepared, ultimately, to reveal what we now have in our New Testament: all that Jesus had taught, the truth about Him into which they will be led, and in addition things that were and are still to come.[7] The grand design is this: the Father speaks the word to the Son, who hears it; the Son speaks the word to the apostles, who receive it; the apostles (in the power of the Spirit) speak the word to us, and we believe it.[8] It is this pattern that lies behind the absolute conviction of the apostles that when they speak it is the word of God that is communicated and received.

This is the chief reason why, although seeing himself as "one born out of due time" (1 Cor. 15:8), Paul defends his apostleship with great vigor. Like the other apostles, he received the word of Christ not from man but from God; not even from the other apostles but through "a revelation of Jesus Christ." Therefore, when he preaches or writes, it is the word of the Lord. Thus, in Thessalonica he preached "the word of the Lord" (1 Thess. 1:8). He therefore rejoiced to be able to write later: "We also thank God without ceasing, because when you received the word of God which you heard from us, you welcomed it not as the word of men, but as it is in truth, the word of God, which also effectively works in you who believe" (1 Thess. 2:13).

---

6. He is the *allos paraklētos* of John 14:16. In this context, *allos*, although not always to be distinguished from *heteros*, clearly indicates not "another of a different kind," but "another of the same kind."

7. See John 14:26; 16:12–15; 15:26, respectively. These, in fact, are the constitutive elements of the documents of the New Testament, and in that sense Jesus has an apostolic canon in view in His promise prophecies. I have discussed this at greater length in Sinclair B. Ferguson, *From the Mouth of God* (Edinburgh: Banner of Truth, 2014), 14–17, 28–38.

8. The sequence is clearly laid out by Jesus in John 17:8, 14–19, 20.

But Paul is able to take this principle—that through the Spirit the preaching of the word of God given to the apostles is itself the word of God, indeed God's voice from God's mouth—one step further. When the word of God is preached in the power of the Spirit, the voice of Christ is heard. People hear Christ. He continues His prophetic office by preaching Himself through the preaching of the Word. Ultimately Christ is not only the worship leader. He is also the preacher. Two other passages in Paul provide further insight here.

Romans 10:13–15

Here, in his positioning of preachers and preaching in the purposes of God, Paul expounds Joel 2:32 by means of a catechism: "For 'everyone who calls on the name of the Lord will be saved.' How then will they call on him in whom they have not believed? *And how are they to believe in him of whom they have never heard?* And how are they to hear without someone preaching? And how are they to preach unless they are sent?" (Rom. 10:13–15 ESV, emphasis added).

Here, the English Standard Version footnote to verse 14b,[9] along with other translators and interpreters, suggests (rightly, in my view) that Paul's words be translated, "How are they to *believe Him whom* they have not heard?" rather than "How are they to believe *in* Him *of* whom they have not heard?"

This is consistent grammatically.[10] Furthermore, it is also consistent with the realities of conversion found in the New Testament narratives and in Christian experience. On the Emmaus road, as Jesus preaches Himself from the Old Testament, He opens the hearts of a couple of travelers to hear His voice—although they do not immediately recognize Him. At the riverside in Philippi, as Paul now speaks about Jesus, Jesus Himself through the word (not apart from it) opens Lydia's heart.

Throughout the ages this is how Christians have experienced and described coming to faith:

> I heard the voice of Jesus say,
> "Come unto Me and rest;
> Lay down, thou weary one, lay down
> Thy head upon My breast."

---

9. Italicized above.

10. The verb "to hear," *akouō*, takes the genitive of the object. Thus "of whom," while a possible translation, is less likely than "whom."

I came to Jesus as I was,
Weary and worn and sad;
I found in Him a resting place,
And He has made me glad.

I heard the voice of Jesus say,
"Behold, I freely give
The living water; thirsty one,
Stoop down, and drink, and live."

I came to Jesus, and I drank
Of that life-giving stream;
My thirst was quenched, my soul revived,
And now I live in Him.[11]

Here Horatius Bonar is describing something more than simply, "I read or heard read Matthew 11:28–30 and John 7:37–39." He is speaking about the mystery of the word coming alive to us—or better, our coming alive to the word—the regeneration and illumination that takes place through the word.[12] He is saying, "I heard Christ—but not with the physical hearing of the ears; rather, I heard Him by the spiritual hearing of the heart through the words of Scripture—yes, 'I heard the voice of Jesus say, "Come unto Me and rest."' He called me and I came."

Ephesians 2:14–18

There is another striking illustration of this in Paul's words in Ephesians 2:14–16:

For He Himself is our peace, who has made both one, and has broken down the middle wall of separation, having abolished in His flesh the enmity, that is, the law of commandments contained in ordinances, so as to create in Himself one new man from the two, thus making peace, and that He might reconcile them both to God in one body through the cross, thereby putting to death the enmity.

These words occur in Paul's exposition of how Jewish and Gentile believers become one new community in Christ. But then the apostle adds in verses 17 and 18: "And He came and preached peace to you who were afar off and

---

11. Horatius Bonar, "I Heard the Voice of Jesus Say," public domain.
12. See James 1:18; 1 Peter 1:23.

to those who were near. For through Him we both have access by one Spirit to the Father."

Notice the movement here. First, Paul has described the finished work of Christ. He refers to what has already been accomplished on the cross. But then, beyond that, following the completion of Christ's work for peace, Paul says that He "came and preached peace" to the Ephesians ("you who were afar off" is semitechnical language to describe Gentiles).

So the question arises: *When* did Jesus do this? When did He visit Ephesus to preach? The answer: when Paul came to preach Jesus Christ and Him crucified. In Paul's preaching the One who was and is the content of the gospel was also present, by His Spirit, as the preacher of the gospel. When Christ preaches Himself to us and offers Himself to us in the word, and by these means the Spirit opens the eyes of our understanding and unstops our heretofore deaf ears, then we hear His voice, recognize it, and follow Him.

In systematic theological terms, this is simply a microscopic view of the older Reformed doctrine of effectual calling, but now expressed in Christological and Christocentric terms and not isolated from Christ in terms of an abstractable element in the *ordo salutis*. In homiletical terms, however, it is a perspective that carries enormous power to transform and recalibrate our entire view of what happens when we preach the Word.

It also helps us to gain perspective on what happens in, through, and under biblical preaching and enhances, if not quite explains, what D. Martyn Lloyd-Jones referred to as its "romance."[13] If the word converts, what it does, in essence, is to bring us through faith to true worship.

Presumably, over a ministry of any length, all preachers have the experience of expounding a passage that seems to sear the conscience, expose sin, and bring us all down low before the sheer majesty of God—and during the exposition sees dear old Mrs. Macdonald, the pensioner, who is crippled with arthritis and preserves her energy on Saturday just to get to Lord's Day worship; or catches the eye of Sarah Shelton, newly widowed; or dear John Overton, whose life story has been so full of tragedy. We want the pulpit to have a trapdoor with a switch we can flick and then disappear through rather than go to the door to shake hands with these loved ones. How very sore this must be for them! They needed comfort, gentleness, and tender encouragement, and we have been engaged in conscience ripping.

---

13. D. Martyn Lloyd-Jones, *Preaching and Preachers* (London: Hodder and Stoughton, 1971), 297–300.

What then explains Mrs. Macdonald taking our hand, smiling gently, and saying, "Thank you, that was so helpful to me; it was just what I needed to hear"? Or John Overton saying, "Ah, Christ is so good; thank you for the word!" Have they, or we, lost contact? How is it that Mrs. Macdonald could leave "lost in wonder, love, and praise"?

Is there an analysis that makes coherent biblical sense of this and so many similar experiences in preaching? Here is the simple, beautiful, praise-God-for-it explanation: Christ Jesus has been present as the preacher of His own Word. What our people have experienced—and this is why one and the same sermon nourishes and evokes worship in such a variety of people with such a diversity of situations and needs—is the presence of the Lord Jesus Himself preaching His Word. No matter what He is saying, He preaches as the One who loves us, who died for us, who is risen and present among us, and who is able to save to the uttermost all those who come to God through Him (Heb. 7:25). Mrs. Macdonald, Sarah Shelton, and John Overton all heard the voice of their Jesus. They know they can trust Him. They know He knows them through and through and understands. Simply to hear His voice—even if He speaks a word of rebuke (for their suffering has not made them sinless)—is all the encouragement they need.

The anonymous author of Hebrews expresses a similar perspective. For him the kingly and the priestly aspects of Christ's threefold office have both a finished and an unfinished dimension. But the same is true of His prophetic ministry, which He continues to exercise now through the written and preached Word. For him the word of God is not an abstract commodity, mere words as it were—a mere book, a dead letter. No, it is, as Jesus confirmed, the mouth of God (Matt. 4:4 quoting Deut. 8:3). In it what has been written in the past addresses us in the present (Heb. 12:6).

As king, the Lord Jesus continues to rule; as priest, He continues to intercede; as prophet, He continues to preach. Thus Hebrews places in the mouth of Jesus the words of Psalm 22:22: "I will declare Your name to My brethren; in the midst of the assembly I will praise You."

Psalm 22 is well known as a messianic prophecy pointing beyond the psalmist to the sufferings of Christ, opening as it does with the cry of dereliction we hear from the cross (Matt. 27:46; Mark 15:34). But the psalm needs to be read right to the end, because it moves from passion to triumph, from the cross to the resurrection, from the finished work of Christ to His ongoing work, from the prophet whose voice seemed to go unheard in heaven to the prophet in heaven whose voice is heard everywhere on earth.

Here is the scene Hebrews paints for us: as we gather as His congregation, Christ is not ashamed to call us brothers. Indeed, He expounds His Father's name to us: "I will declare Your name to My brethren." Notice too that within this context He leads our worship: "In the midst of the assembly I will praise You."

Yes, Jesus is the worship leader. But He is such because He is the preacher. And He preaches as the One who shared our flesh and blood, who died to taste our death and deliver us from the evil one and to make propitiation for our sins. And all this He did as the One who was tempted as we are (Heb. 2:14–18).

We have a guest preacher this coming Sunday—and for that matter every Sunday: Jesus Himself. Indeed, it would be truer to say we are a guest congregation every Sunday. No matter what the text, Christ's sermon title will be "Jesus Himself"—the subject that requires every verse, chapter, and book in the Bible fully to expound.

When we grasp this, not only are our theology of the gathering of the congregation and the privilege of worship enhanced but the relationship between preaching and worship is clarified. It explains why the human preacher worships—because he himself bows before the preaching of Jesus even while he preaches. He is in awe of his role as His mouthpiece. And such preaching evokes worship—we are in Christ's presence; His voice is heard. Let all within cry "glory!"

The Bible class I attended as a teenager opened every week with us singing:

> Jesus, stand among us
> In thy risen power;
> Let this time of worship
> Be a hallowed hour.[14]

It was some time before I realized what the answer to the question of what He does as He stands among us included: He preaches His own Word, He draws us to Himself, and He shows us that He is always completely adequate to be our Savior. Precisely what the author of Hebrews affirmed!

This perspective carries a very wide variety of implications related to preachers and their preaching. Here we must limit ourselves to considering only two of them.

---

14. William Pennefather (1816–1873), "Jesus, Stand among Us," public domain.

Implications

There is a telling expression that was often on the lips of our spiritual fore-
bears when they identified their spiritual home by saying, for example, "I
sit under X's ministry." We moderns might take umbrage at the minister-
centeredness we perceive in this.[15] But there is a danger that we "throw
out the baby with the bathwater," and, in regretting the minister-centered
description, we forget the posture that is described. For in those days Christians neither spoke of nor thought of preaching as "sitting round" the word
of God; or of preachers who "shared" it; or, for that matter, of clergymen
who gave "talks." All of that would have betrayed to them an anthropo-
centric, horizontal, minimalistic, nondynamic—indeed (paradoxically),
monological—view of preaching. No, they sat "under" the Word because
they believed that the most important thing about preaching was that in and
through it they heard the voice of Christ, bowed before Him, and worshiped
Him. Preaching was not so much the transfer of information (no matter how
insightful), but the reality of submissive communion with Christ. The goal
was not instruction, but adoration.

There is a primary implication here for preachers. To put it in personal
terms, *no one sits "under" my preaching more than I do if I am the preacher.*
For the answer to the question, "Who preaches to the preacher?" is the same
as the answer to the question, "Who preaches to the congregation?" Jesus
Christ. This is why the history of homiletics is punctuated by such adages as
that of John Owen that "I find that those sermons go with most power from
me that came with most power to me." But this does not only mean they
came with power to us before we preach them, important though that may
be; it means *while* we are preaching them. The preacher is a listener even as he
preaches. The weight with which the word of Christ is heard and felt by him
is the measure of the weight of that same word as it is spoken through him.
We sit under our own preaching.

This is the view and experience of preaching that is conducive to worship—and first in the preacher himself. For here the preacher does not lord it

---

15. That said, our modern evangelical subculture may be in danger of simply transfer-
ring this to another level by its "guru centricism," in which our luminaries are ranked, and
we bask in the reflected glow of the one we most appreciate—or at the opposite extreme
seek to demonstrate on our websites, blogs, or Twitter feeds that these men have feet of clay.
Technology can give the appearance of broadening our horizon, but it can easily do so at the
expense of love for and loyalty to our local congregation and its pastor(s). It is not an easy task
for ministers to warn their own congregation, or individuals in it, of such a danger.

over the congregation; he does not use the word as an instrument of his own dispositions or emotions; nor does he give the impression that he is wiser or greater or better than they are. He stands in front of them physically, but he sits beside them spiritually—he is fundamentally the chief listener. Christ preaches to him even as the preacher preaches to them.

Why should this be so conducive to preaching that evokes worship? For the simple reason that such preaching is itself an act of worship. For what is not itself worship cannot serve the ends of worship, nor will it promote it.

That is why the age-old words that I used to hear at the start of every worship service set the tone for everything that followed, including, pre-eminently, the preaching of the Word: "Let us worship God." These words indicated that the pastor-teacher himself was giving himself to the Lord in worship. And that included the sermon. For the later words customarily spoken before the reading of the Scriptures, "Let us hear the word of God," simply intensified the words "Let us worship God." The disappearance of such expressions is usually explained in terms of informality or not being hidebound by tradition. But by losing the words, we may also have lost the theology enshrined in them.

A second implication worth highlighting is as follows: *Worship is the expression of the whole person, and thus, to a great extent, involves the affections.* Thus, preaching that expresses the worship of the human preacher, if it is to be conducive to this element in both individual and congregational worship, must come through and engage the affections of the hearers. Put in christological terms, this, above all, requires the preacher to be familiar with Christ as the Affectionate One.

This was a central element in Jonathan Edwards's homiletical thinking. Defending the Great Awakening against its severest critics, he wrote:

> I think an exceeding affectionate way of preaching about the great things of religion, has in itself no tendency to beget false apprehensions of them; but on the contrary a much greater tendency to beget true apprehensions of them, than a moderate, dull, indifferent way of speaking of 'em.... And I don't think ministers are to be blamed for raising the affections of their hearers too high.... I should think myself in the way of my duty to raise the affections of my hearers as high as possibly I can, provided that they are affected with nothing but the truth, and with affections that are not disagreeable to the nature of what they are affected with. I know it has long been fashionable to despise a very earnest and pathetical way of preaching...but I humbly conceive it has

been for a want of understanding, or duly considering human nature, that such preaching has been thought to have the greatest tendency to answer the ends of preaching; and the experience of the present and past ages abundantly confirms the same.[16]

Clearly in Edwards's capacious and inquisitive mind there was no contradiction between rigorous intellectual clarity and deeply experienced affections. He certainly understood the principle that Thomas Chalmers would later describe in his famous sermon on Colossians 3:1, "The Expulsive Power of a New Affection," because he realized that the greatest commandment to love the Lord our God with all our heart, soul, mind, and strength involved the whole person. In the older faculty psychology (within which Edwards operated), love—which is the *sine qua non* of the worship of the triune Lord—involved both mind and affections, the reasonable and the volitional aspects of the soul united in the happiest of marriages—the understanding grasping the beauty of God and His way of salvation, the will embracing it through the affections. Edwards was by no means original or novel in this emphasis. He himself drew on the so-called affectionate preaching in the Puritan tradition, especially of Richard Sibbes[17] and John Flavel.[18]

Edwards does not seem to have been familiar with the work of William Fenner. In many ways his *Treatise of the Affections*[19] provides a landmark for preachers. Almost a century before Edwards's *Religious Affections* saw the light of day, Fenner affirmed in the course of his notable exposition of the important role of the affections that "ministers must labour to stir up the affections

16. Jonathan Edwards, *Some Thoughts Concerning the Present Revival of Religion in New England* (1742), in *The Works of Jonathan Edwards*, volume 4, *The Great Awakening*, ed. C. C. Goen (New Haven, Conn.: Yale University Press, 1972), 386–87.

17. Richard Sibbes (1577–1635) was a student at St. John's College, Cambridge, and was later lecturer at Holy Trinity Church, preacher at Gray's Inn (one of the Inns of Court in London), and from 1626 also master of St. Catherine's Hall in Cambridge. The imprint of his ministry was left on many of the most significant Puritan leaders, and his works represent the finest of the Puritan tradition of pastoral preaching combining the mind of an able scholar with the heart of a true pastor.

18. John Flavel (1627–1691) was a student at University College, Oxford, and later minister in Diptford and then at Dartmouth and suffered during the Great Ejection of 1662. His works are an outstanding example of Reformed experimental pastoral theology.

19. The work has a characteristically delicious Puritan title: *A Treatise of the Affections, or The Souls Pulse whereby a Christian may know whether he be living or dying: Together with a lively description of their nature, signes, and symptoms: As also directing men to a right use of them* (London, 1657). William Fenner was a fellow of Pembroke College in Cambridge and later rector of Rockford in Essex.

of the hearers." Not only so, but he provided directives to ministers to help them to do so.

It is certainly important for preachers and for the health of our preaching to recover a sense that the Lord we worship is an affectionate God and that we therefore cannot fully love Him apart from the reordering, restoring, and recalibrating of the affections in our worship. While in many quarters the role of the affections has been too long neglected, voices are beginning to be heard again that recapture elements of the older understanding. But since this is still occasional, and perhaps largely due to a revived interest in Edwards's work, it may be useful to conclude this essay by highlighting an example of the older tradition.

Fenner sees the Emmaus road narrative describing how, through Christ's exposition of His own word, hearts are given up to the object of their affections as they burn in Christ's presence. This is ultimately what is in view in preaching and is the *sine qua non* of worship.

But how is this to be encouraged? A few of Fenner's reflections must bring our analysis to a close.

1. Affections are raised, fixed, and enflamed when ministers "preach to the life," that is, when their exposition explains, describes, and expounds reality as it is. As James VI and I[20] noted of one Puritan, "He preaches as if death were at my back."

2. For this to become a reality in our own ministry of the word, we preachers must be full of affection. "Affection in the speaker is likely to beget affections in the hearer."[21] Fenner distinguishes this from mere externals in preaching. It is not a matter of personality type or communication skills, certainly not "emotionalism." As Calvin notes, there are preachers who thus preach, but they leave their hearers cold and unmoved because they perceive that what they hear is only surface emotion and not truly the affections of the reasonable and volitional soul.

3. Preachers must be marked by godliness in their own lives. Only in this way will their own affections be pure and worshipful, and only

---

20. James VI of Scotland succeeded to the throne of England in 1603 on the death of Elizabeth I, thus uniting the crowns of Scotland (of which he was James VI) and England (where he became James I).

21. Fenner, *Treatise of the Affections*, 50.

thus will they be appropriate vessels through whom Christ will touch and move the affections of their hearers. This is not merely a matter of style but of quality of life.

4. Intriguingly, Fenner adds that affectionate preaching will be expressed in the voice. Here he stands consciously in a long line of rhetorical theorists stretching back at least to Augustine who acknowledged that they could not explain this relationship, but they knew that it was the case. Fenner held that when the preacher's affections are moved, this will become evident in the vehicle by which he expresses them to others.

5. Fenner also notes that affections are expressed and evoked through the preacher's actions in his preaching—admitting his own limitations precisely here.[22]

These emphases certainly serve to stimulate reflection four centuries later. But in a sense, they simply bring us back to our point of origin. Worship is the activity of every aspect of our being—body, mind, will, and affections. In this context one of the preacher's burdens is the extent to which the Lord Jesus Himself desires to speak through our preaching of His word in order to make His people conscious of His presence and to bring them to bow in love and praise before Him. And like worship, of which it is a central element, preaching is an act of our whole being and of our worship. Our whole being as preachers, therefore, including our affections, must first be subdued by Christ, must be sanctified by His word, and must be sensitive to His Spirit. Then, not only in preparation for preaching or as a response following preaching, but in, under, and throughout the preaching of the word, our own affections, as well as those of our hearers, will be stirred. Thus, both preacher and hearers alike—indeed, all who are "in His temple" will "cry 'Glory!'" The answer to the first question in the "Preacher's Shorter Catechism" will then become clear: What is the chief end of preaching? The chief end of preaching is that we may glorify God and enjoy Him forever.

When that is experienced, the deep relationship between preaching and worship becomes more than theory. For like much else, as our forefathers used to say, the reality of such worship is "better felt than telt."

---

22. While this will seem artificial to some readers, it is worth noting that in the early editions of C. H. Spurgeon's famous *Lectures to My Students*, he had included woodcuts diagramming gesticulations.

PART 3
The Motivation of Preaching

CHAPTER 8

The Aim of Preaching: The Glory of God

W. Robert Godfrey

One passion of the heart and ministry of Dr. Steven J. Lawson is the glory of God. For him, one of the great aims of preaching is to glorify God, and in that conviction he is following the teaching of the Scriptures and the practice of the great Protestant Reformers. The Scriptures again and again explicitly show that the preaching and teaching of the truth as it is in Jesus Christ lead the people of God to glorify Him. Where faith responds to the work of Jesus, there we find praise and glory given to God. This response to Jesus remains the ultimate aim of every preacher.

One important example of such preaching and teaching is to be found in Luke 13:10–35, where we are shown that the proper response to the words and miracles of Jesus is to glorify God. In honoring Dr. Lawson, it is surely appropriate to exposit a passage of Scripture to show that these truths come directly from the Word of God. At the same time, since Dr. Lawson stands in the great tradition of Reformed preachers, it will also be fitting to refer to John Calvin's understanding of this text. Calvin was one of the great preachers of the Reformation and therefore one of the influences on all later Reformed expositors and preachers.

Luke 13:10–17 leads us to glorify God by beginning with Jesus teaching on the Sabbath in a synagogue. As Jesus is expounding the Scriptures, He sees a woman who had been crippled for eighteen years. He speaks to her: "Woman, you are loosed from your infirmity" (v. 12). Then He touches her and heals her. This healing produces strong reactions—positive from the woman, but negative from the ruler of the synagogue. The woman glorifies God, but the leader of the synagogue criticizes Jesus, indirectly, for healing on the Sabbath.

These reactions lead to further teaching from Jesus on the character of His kingdom (Luke 13:18–35). He makes clear that His realm is present wherever He brings grace and liberation. One day the kingdom will be complete, perfect, and glorious, but now it is already present in His blessing on this daughter of Abraham. The kingdom is not primarily present in the miracle but rather in the relationship and blessing that Jesus as King establishes for this woman, His subject, through His words and actions. Jesus's teaching and miracles are interconnected in carrying His message. His miracles are a visible means of teaching: Jesus came to save and liberate His people, which we see in action when Jesus heals the woman. The effect of Jesus's actions is that the liberated woman glorifies God: "She was made straight, and glorified God" (v. 13). When the kingdom comes in its fullness, then all His own will fully bless and glorify Him forever.

This passage in Luke 13 is one part of the preaching ministry of Jesus, and we need to see it in its larger context to understand it properly. Jesus was a preacher from the beginning of His ministry to the end, just before His ascension. Preaching was one of His greatest works, and in his gospel Luke presents the whole story of Jesus in what could be called a series of sermons. Luke structures his telling of the good news of Jesus in a way that shows us Jesus the preacher. He begins his account of the public ministry of Jesus in a synagogue in Nazareth, where Jesus reads from Isaiah:

> "The Spirit of the LORD is upon Me,
> Because He has anointed Me
> To preach the gospel to the poor;
> He has sent Me to heal the brokenhearted,
> To proclaim liberty to the captives
> And recovery of sight to the blind,
> To set at liberty those who are oppressed;
> To proclaim the acceptable year of the LORD." (4:18–19)

This text can be translated more literally to show the grammatical relationship of elements of the text in this way:

> "The Spirit of the Lord is upon me
>   because
> He has anointed me to preach good news to the poor.
>   He has sent me to proclaim to the captives deliverance
>   and to the blind recovery of sight,
>   to send for the oppressed deliverance,
>   to proclaim the acceptable year of the Lord."

Luke wanted his original hearers and us to linger over this text and particularly to see its connection to Jesus when He simply preached: "Today this Scripture is fulfilled in your hearing" (4:21). Jesus is the Messiah anointed by the Spirit; He is the preacher and the liberator prophesied by Isaiah. In His entire ministry, Jesus is the Spirit-filled Messiah, the preacher, and the deliverer. But Luke also uses this text to organize the material of his gospel and to highlight aspects of Jesus's fulfillment of Isaiah's prophecy. Luke stresses Jesus as the Messiah who preaches good news in 4:20–9:17 and then stresses Jesus as the Messiah who delivers the oppressed in 9:37–19:27. The Father's identification of Jesus as His Messiah and Son at the transfiguration links these two sections (9:18–36).

Luke presents the liberating work of Jesus in his second section of the gospel in a variety of ways and from different perspectives. At the heart of this section Luke places Jesus's healing and His teaching on the kingdom of God (13:10–35). Luke's presentation here really has three points, for Luke too was a preacher! First, Luke shows us the grace of King Jesus (13:10–17); second, he shows us the character of the growth of His kingdom (13:20–30); and third, he shows us the greatness of King Jesus (13:31–35).

The Grace of the King

> Declare His glory among the nations,
> His wonders among all peoples.
> —Psalm 96:3

Liberating (Luke 13:10–13)

As God's King and Messiah, Jesus shows His liberating grace while teaching in a synagogue one Sabbath. He sees a crippled woman who had been oppressed for eighteen years by her affliction. She is bent over and unable to straighten herself up. Jesus calls to her, speaks to her words of liberation, touches her, and immediately heals her.

In this miracle Jesus clearly shows both His power and His love for His people. As Calvin reflected:

> In this miracle, as in others, Christ shows both His power and His grace...for He proclaims authoritatively that liberation lies in His hand.... The point of His saying that the people glorified God is to teach us that this heavenly benefit was open and plain. It was no obscure

work, on which people could argue for and against, but provided a full and sure basis for praising God.[1]

However little people recognize Jesus for who He is, His works bear abundant testimony to His identity: "The works of the LORD are great, studied by all who have pleasure in them" (Ps. 111:2).

This poor, afflicted daughter of Abraham recognizes that God has visited her in this healing. We do not know how fully or minimally she understood the person and work of Jesus at this time, but we do know that she glorified God for her healing. In response to the miraculous work of Jesus, she praises God. Her reaction calls all of us to join with her in glorifying God.

Libeled (Luke 13:14)

The woman's response of thanks to God is not shared by all, however. The ruler of the synagogue, who had responsibility for what happened there, is furious. We do not know exactly what he thought of Jesus, but he clearly did not accept that He was King or Messiah. Instead he saw Jesus as a breaker of the law and a violator of the Sabbath.

Calvin recognized the spirit that underlays this criticism. He wrote: "Now, although this ungodly critic is dumb with shame, yet we see that Christ never did any such wonderful work without the wicked making it an excuse to malign Him. It is no wonder if Satan bends all His efforts to destroy the glory of Christ, for he does not cease to spread his mists everywhere to obscure the godly activities of believers."[2] Rather than see the glory of God in Jesus's healing, this ruler rejected the evident display of God's work, clothing his rejection in religious indignation.

The ruler presents what many of his hearers may have believed was a sound, theological reaction: there are six days in the week in which the work of healing may be performed, but the Sabbath is a day of rest from work. Calvin commented appropriately about the foolishness of this ruler:

> Why does he not drive them [all the people] away from the synagogue in case they violated the Sabbath? Why does he not command them to cease from all the practices of religion? Since men are only forbidden to do their own works on the Sabbath, how wrong it is to tie down God's

---

1. John Calvin, *A Harmony of the Gospels Matthew, Mark and Luke,* trans. T. H. L. Parker (Grand Rapids: Eerdmans, 1972), 2:97.

2. Calvin, *Harmony,* 2:98.

grace!… What was the point of that holy assembling save that believers might beg God's aid and help?[3]

Calvin sees both the true meaning of the Sabbath institution and the blindness of this ruler of the synagogue.

We know that Jesus always kept the law perfectly and did not need instruction in truth from this ruler. How would Jesus respond to this unfair criticism?

Lacerating (Luke 13:15–17)

Jesus responds very sharply indeed, labeling the ruler a hypocrite. This lacerating appellation means more than one who says one thing and does another. It probably rests on a Hebrew word that carries with it the idea of pollution. This ruler is not just insincere and corrupt, but a polluter of those around him. Far from upholding the law, he has misrepresented and corrupted it.

That day Jesus spoke to all those there who would have agreed with this ruler, showing them that they valued animals more than they did God's covenant people. They would work to save a beast, but not to save a daughter of Abraham. Is not the saving work of God the essence of the Sabbath? We rest to reflect on the work of God. Jesus understands the Sabbath, where the legalists miss its true meaning altogether.

By these words Jesus shames and humiliates those who oppose Him. They have no answer for His justification and defense of His actions. For in both His liberating healing and His liberating teaching the people see His glory in His works and rejoice. Here indeed is the correct and necessary response to the works of God in His Christ.

The Growth of the Kingdom

> All Your works shall praise You, O LORD,
> And Your saints shall bless You.
> They shall speak of the glory of Your kingdom,
> And talk of Your power,
> To make known to the sons of men His mighty acts,
> And the glorious majesty of His kingdom.
> —Psalm 145:10–12

---

3. Calvin, *Harmony*, 2:97.

Pervasive Growth (Luke 13:20–21)

Luke records, "Then [Jesus] said, 'What is the kingdom of God like? And to what shall I compare it?'" (v. 18). Jesus has not changed the subject from healing to the kingdom of God. Rather, He is showing that the meaning of His kingdom is suggested, indeed revealed, in this healing. Where the King exercises His royal authority, His kingdom is present.

This healing miracle in one sense is a glorious and objective demonstration of the power of Jesus. But in another sense we can say that it is a small matter. One person, whose name we do not know, in a world of sick people is healed at a place and time unknown to us. Jesus wants to explain how this one act in its two distinct senses illustrates the kingdom of God.

Jesus uses two similes, one of a mustard seed and the other of leaven in bread, to present the nature of His kingdom. In the first He seems to stress that the kingdom is small in its beginning but grows large enough for birds to nest in it. The point of the simile is not that the kingdom will grow to be large, powerful, and wealthy, but that despite its initial smallness it will grow large enough to be a home for many.

The second simile is comparable, but with a slightly different emphasis. The leaven in bread does make it somewhat bigger, but the point is that the leaven permeates the whole. So the stress is not that the kingdom will fill the world, but will be throughout the world. The kingdom will not be limited to one place or people, but will be everywhere.

So the kingdom is indeed like the healing of the crippled woman: wonderful and insignificant to the world at the same time. The kingdom will develop out of the work and teaching of Jesus in the life of each one to whom Jesus comes, just as has happened in the life of this woman. For each one it is wonderful and, at the same time, a small matter in the eyes of the world.

Calvin applies this teaching of Jesus to the struggles of the Reformation churches in his own day in a way that also helps us face the weaknesses of the churches in our day:

> In these parables Christ encourages His disciples so that they may not shrink back in offense at the lowly beginnings of the Gospel. We see how irreligious men in their arrogance despise the Gospel, even laugh at it, because it is brought by obscure and unknown ministers, and because it is not received at once by universal applause, but has only a few followers and those mostly insignificant and mean. And so the weak come to despair of the outcome when they assess it by the beginnings. But it was deliberately that the Lord started His Kingdom from weak and lowly

beginnings, so that the unlooked for progress might glorify His power the better.[4]

Today still the weakness of Christ's ministers in their work serves only to glorify Christ.

Personal Growth (Luke 13:22–30)

Luke continues the story, showing us Jesus setting out for Jerusalem. Jesus knows that it is necessary for Him to die there as the great saving work that lays the foundation of His kingdom and new covenant. Luke continues the theme of the character of the kingdom in Jesus's response to a question: "Lord, are there few who are saved?" (v. 23). This question, at first glance, may seem surprising and unrelated to the context. But, on reflection, in part it probably arose from the similes in the passage that are related to the size of the kingdom. More particularly we should probably see this question as subtly hostile toward Jesus. Almost all of the questions put to Jesus between the Transfiguration and His triumphal entry into Jerusalem are antagonistic— the oppressors against the liberator. Perhaps the questioner hoped that if Jesus made His kingdom sound very narrow and difficult to enter that He would alienate many of His followers. Conversely, if He made the kingdom too easy to enter, He might have disillusioned many who were strict among His followers.

As He often does, Jesus seems to answer the question that should have been asked rather than the one actually asked. Jesus, in effect, tells His listeners not to be concerned in the first place about whether the kingdom will have few or many in it. Rather, He tells them to be sure that they are in it. He is really saying, "You strive to enter it rather than worrying about others."

The call to strive from Jesus may well have had an ironic dimension to it. The hostile questioners were likely strict observers of the law of Moses according to the interpretation of the Pharisees. Their lives were lives of striving and earning merit. They saw themselves as workers of righteousness. But Jesus strongly rebukes them. They have not been workers of righteousness, but workers of evil (v. 27). Jesus calls them to a different kind of work—namely, to recognize and believe that Jesus is Messiah, Son of God, and true King. So far, they have not listened to Him, believed His word, or obeyed Him.

---

4. Calvin, *Harmony*, 2:79.

Jesus makes clear that the entrance to the kingdom is by a narrow gate through which only those dedicated to the King will enter. Many would like to inherit the kingdom but do not listen to their true master and Lord. They do not come when He calls, but will only come according to their own timing. They will say that they are His people and that He ate, drank, and taught among them. But He will say that they are not His people—indeed, that He does not know where they are from. Like the ruler of the synagogue, they are workers of iniquity, rejecting the Messiah and rejected by Him. Being from Israel does not ensure entrance into the kingdom.

The loss of the kingdom will lead to horrible anguish among those who are rejected. A great part of that suffering will be to see the holy patriarchs and prophets enjoying the kingdom without them. But it will not only be patriarchs and prophets who inherit the kingdom. Many others from all over the world will also come to be part of the kingdom. Jesus seems to be saying that while many of the old covenant people will be excluded from Messiah's realm, many Gentiles will be included. These Israelites were first but will be last because they rejected Jesus. These Gentiles were last but will be first because they believed in Jesus.

So what is the answer to the question that was posed to Jesus about whether the number saved would be few? The answer is that in one sense there will be few, and in another sense there will be many. Few of those who expected to be in the kingdom will be there, but many who were expected to be excluded from the kingdom will be there. For Jesus the key matter then and today is that each one who hears His call should strive to enter, trusting the word of the King.

Again Calvin applies this text in a most helpful way, reminding us that we should not necessarily expect a crowd to accompany us into the kingdom:

> By these words, He intended to move His folk away from that foolish curiosity which hinders and complicates many who keep looking around to see whether other companions are joining them, as if they could only gain salvation in a great crowd.... This is added, to avoid our empty hopes letting us down, if we had imagined that a crowd of companions would help us, for under the gentle blandishments of the flesh, many promise themselves an easy access to life, and constantly indulge themselves.[5]

---

5. Calvin, *Harmony*, 1:234.

The narrow gate means that it is not by counting noses that we will establish the truth.

The Greatness of the King

His glory is great in Your salvation;
Honor and majesty You have placed upon Him.
—Psalm 21:5

Work to Complete (Luke 13:31–32)
Luke continues: Jesus is warned that Herod wants to kill Him, but as the great and true King of His people, He is not at all intimidated. Jesus knows Herod for what he is—not a true king in Israel but a tyrant, deceiver, and murderer. In any case Jesus knows that Herod is no real threat to Him. As God's true Son and King, He has work to do and will do it. His current work is to show Himself as the liberator of His people in teaching the truth, casting out demons, and curing them of their diseases. In due course He will complete His work, and Herod will not be able to interfere in any way. In referring to "the third day" and to finishing His work (v. 32), He clearly foreshadows and anticipates His future death and resurrection.

Death to Die (Luke 13:33)
The work that He has to complete in Jerusalem is to die there. His death has been prepared for and typified by the death of the earlier prophets. His death is, of course, the ultimate rejection by Jerusalem and her leaders of the true Messiah. As they have always rejected the true prophets of God, so they will reject this final prophet. Jesus does not elaborate here on the meaning and effect of His death in Jerusalem, but all Christian readers of Luke's gospel know the significance and necessity of this death for the salvation of the world. Jesus saves as substitute and sacrifice, bearing the full wrath of God for all the sins of all His people.

Sermon to Preach (Luke 13:34–35)
Jesus shows again the importance of preaching in His work. He addresses the city of Jerusalem with passion and concern. Here Jerusalem, as the capital of Israel, stands for the whole old covenant establishment, and Jesus reminds the people of their appalling history. Repeatedly God had sent His prophets to them to remind them of their covenant obligations, and repeatedly the prophets had been violently rejected.

Calvin recognizes Israel's history of sin: "Christ is not reproving any particular murder, but a city so steeped in the habit that it did not cease slaying as many prophets as were sent. The particle is used as an epithet, as if Christ had said, you should have been the faithful guardian of the Word of God, teacher of heavenly wisdom, example of faith and obedience—but you are a prophet-slayer, so that now you have caught the habit of drinking their blood."[6] In this remarkable observation, Calvin reminds all of us of the great responsibility of being faithful guardians of God's Word.

In this sermon Jesus significantly implies that He is the divine preacher whose Spirit has been present in all of Israel's prophets through the centuries. His words "how often" (v. 34) seem to reach beyond the years of His human life to the whole history of Israel. This understanding that the Spirit of Jesus was at work among the people of Israel before His incarnation is frequent in the New Testament. For example, Paul, writing of Israel wandering in the wilderness, stated: "For they drank of that spiritual Rock that followed them, and that Rock was Christ" (1 Cor. 10:4). Similarly, Jude wrote: "But I want to remind you, though you once knew this, that the Lord, having saved the people out of the land of Egypt, afterward destroyed those who did not believe" (v. 5). (After comparing ancient Greek manuscripts, this Jude text is better translated in the English Standard Version: "Now I want to remind you, although you once fully knew it, that Jesus, who saved a people out of the land of Egypt, afterward destroyed those who did not believe.") Jesus indeed, throughout the history of Israel, sought to gather His people to Himself.

The allusions to Jesus's divinity continue when He compares Himself to a hen protecting her chicks "as a hen gathers her brood under her wings" (v. 34). The image of finding shelter under wings is a reference to God and His protective care of His people in the Old Testament (Pss. 17:8; 36:7; 61:4; 91:4; cf. Deut. 32:11). Here again Jesus presents Himself as fulfilling a divine role.

As divine preacher and prophet, Jesus now appeals again to His recalcitrant people. His call is that they would respond to Him and enter His kingdom and share in its blessings. He comes to gather them to Himself—that is the message of His public ministry and the appeal of all the preachers whom He has sent into the world since His resurrection. The sense is very much what the prophets always preached: "Say to them: 'As I live,' says the Lord GOD, 'I have no pleasure in the death of the wicked, but that the wicked

---

6. Calvin, *Harmony*, 3:67.

turn from his way and live. Turn, turn from your evil ways! For why should you die, O house of Israel?'" (Ezek. 33:11).

The stress of this appeal is on human responsibility. God sends forth this well-meant offer of salvation to all, but they must respond. They must not reject and repudiate the word preached to them. When the mother hen comes to gather her chicks, they must not run away. The children of Jerusalem have run away from their Lord and Savior. Their destruction is their own responsibility alone.

Calvin gives eloquent expression to this divine care for God's old covenant people:

> If God's grace had been rejected at Jerusalem and nothing more, it was already inexcusable ingratitude, but seeing that God's approach to the Jews had been to attract them with gentleness and friendship, and His kindness brought Him no success, the proud insult He charged them with was greatly aggravated.... By this He means that whenever the Word of God is put before us He bares His breast to us with maternal kindness, and not content with that comes down to the humble affection of a hen fostering her chicks.[7]

God's kindness and love are always primary in the gospel appeal.

Calvin indeed shows his passion for us to understand the goodness of God to sinners: "If we consider on the one hand the dread Majesty of God, and on the other our sordid and abject condition, we must with shame come to gasp at the wonder of such great goodness."[8] Of course if many will not gasp in response to the preaching of Jesus, we may not be surprised if they do not gasp in response to our preaching.

Jesus the preacher and prophet pronounces condemnation: "See! Your house is left to you desolate" (13:35). The exact meaning of "house" here is somewhat ambiguous. Jesus's word may allude to several different prophetic passages. In Isaiah 64:11 "house" refers to the temple:

> Our holy and beautiful temple,
> Where our fathers praised You,
> Is burned up with fire;
> And all our pleasant things are laid waste.

---

7. Calvin, *Harmony*, 3:68.
8. Calvin, *Harmony*, 3:68.

In Jeremiah 12:7 "house" refers to the nation as a whole: "I have forsaken My house, I have left My heritage; I have given the dearly beloved of My soul into the hand of her enemies." In Jeremiah 22:5 "house" refers to the city of Jerusalem: "'But if you will not hear these words, I swear by Myself,' says the LORD, 'that this house shall become a desolation.'" In a sense it all comes to the same thing. This condemnation, paralleling Matthew 23:38, spells the end of the old covenant economy. Jesus's kingdom has come to fulfill all the promises to Israel. All that the temple, the city, and the nation have meant and have pointed to are now fulfilled in Jesus. To the extent that the children of Jerusalem have rejected the Messiah, the Messiah rejects them.

Calvin sees this meaning clearly in the text: "So they reckoned the temple as an invincible bastion, as if they sat in God's bastion. Christ contends that they vainly boast themselves of God's presence, for their crimes have driven Him away. By calling it your house He indirectly implies it is God's no longer. The temple had been erected with a view that it would cease to be God's abode and resting-place at the coming of Christ."[9] As they have not understood the true meaning of their law, so they have not understood the meaning of their temple and its sacrifices.

At the end of this sermon He reminds His listeners after this condemnation that they will not see Him again until they hail Him as Messiah, citing Psalm 118:26. This psalm was regularly used at the Passover and was seen as a prophecy of the coming Messiah. This verse would indeed be called out by Jesus's disciples at the triumphal entry into Jerusalem (Luke 19:38).

Psalm 118 is a great celebration of the coming Messiah and of the love of God for His people. It begins and ends with praise for the covenant love of God: "Oh, give thanks to the LORD, for He is good! For His mercy endures forever" (Ps. 118:1, 29). This psalm also stresses that the entrance to God's kingdom is for the righteous—that is to say, those who trust in God:

> Open to me the gates of righteousness;
> I will go through them,
> And I will praise the LORD.
> This is the gate of the LORD,
> Through which the righteous shall enter.
>
> I will praise You,
> For You have answered me,
> And have become my salvation. (Ps. 118:19–21)

---

9. Calvin, *Harmony*, 3:70.

The gate of righteousness must be the narrow gate of which Jesus has spoken.

This conclusion to the sermon may be interpreted in two quite different ways. One way is to see Jesus as saying that those who have rejected Him will one day be forced to confess Him. This interpretation sees His words as expressing the truth found in other texts. One is Philippians 2:10–11: "At the name of Jesus every knee should bow, of those in heaven, and of those on earth, and of those under the earth, and that every tongue should confess that Jesus Christ is Lord, to the glory of God the Father." Another is Romans 14:11, which cites Isaiah 45:23:

> For it is written:
> "As I live, says the LORD,
> Every knee shall bow to Me,
> And every tongue shall confess to God."

This is also the way in which Calvin takes the text:

> We see how Christ in a figurative way criticizes their empty hypocrisy, for as if they ardently longed for the promised salvation they sang daily from the Psalm, "Blessed is he that cometh in the name of the Lord" (Psalm 118:26), and at the same time they mocked the Redeemer offered to them. He says that He will not come to them until they cry out in fear—too late—at the sight of His terrible Majesty, "truly He is the Son of God." This threat goes to all who scorn the Gospel, especially those who falsely profess His Name while they reject His teaching.[10]

Alternatively, some take these words of Jesus in a positive sense. Then they would mean that while the old economy with Israel has come to an end, still every child of Jerusalem who turns to the Messiah to acknowledge and bless Him will be saved. On this understanding, the close of this message would be a call to faith.

Perhaps Jesus has an intentional ambiguity here, for both interpretations present biblical truths that are found elsewhere. Every mouth will one day be forced to confess that He is Lord. And everyone who calls on the name of the Lord in the day of salvation will be saved.

What is clear is that the proper and necessary response to Jesus is to bless Him. That brings us back to the aim of preaching: to glorify God. To bless God is to glorify Him. Those who hear the word of God through His

---

10. Calvin, *Harmony*, 3:71.

preachers are called to faith and repentance, and those who believe will glorify God in their words and lives. Here, indeed, is the aim of preaching. It
was the aim of Jesus in His preaching, and it must be the aim of all faithful
preachers of His Word until He comes again—at which time every tongue
will indeed proclaim: "Blessed is He who comes in the name of the Lord!"

CHAPTER 9

The Foundation of Preaching: The Cross of Christ

John J. Murray

The biblical understanding of a preacher is that he is a man with a message, a herald. Paul says that he has been appointed a preacher, or herald, of the gospel (1 Tim. 2:7; 2 Tim. 1:11). But what is his message? "We preach [herald] Christ crucified" (1 Cor. 1:23). He makes clear that the foundation of his preaching is the cross of the Lord Jesus Christ. We need to look at the various considerations that make it essential for the preacher to have the cross of Christ as the foundation of his message.

The Cross of Christ: The Message That God Gives

The preacher is a herald whose primary concern is to deliver the message as he has received it. He preaches because God has commanded him. The basic principle as far as the message is concerned is clearly expressed in the words of the Lord to Jonah: "Arise, go to Nineveh, that great city, and preach to it the message that I tell you" (Jonah 3:2). God's message was given to prophets and apostles by direct revelation. After them, the message for preaching was committed to the Holy Scriptures. The important thing to consider is that it was given. The preacher is not to invent or originate the message or preach his own opinions. The New Testament command to preach comes from our Lord Himself when He declared to His disciples: "Go into all the world and preach the gospel to every creature" (Mark 16:15). A similar command is found in Matthew 28:19–20.

If the message is in the Bible and if nothing that God has revealed is superfluous, then all of Scripture is important. But surely among all the truths in the Word of God, there are things that are of primary importance. That is what we find in the teaching of the New Testament, especially in the words of the apostle Paul. In writing to the church at Corinth the apostle says:

"For Jews request a sign, and Greeks seek after wisdom; but we preach Christ crucified, to the Jews a stumbling block and to the Greeks foolishness, but to those who are called, both Jews and Greeks, Christ the power of God and the wisdom of God" (1 Cor. 1:22–24). Later on he asserts: "For I determined not to know anything among you except Jesus Christ and Him crucified" (1 Cor. 2:2). In Galatians he says, "But God forbid that I should boast except in the cross of our Lord Jesus Christ, by whom the world has been crucified to me, and I to the world" (Gal. 6:14).

In these passages Paul is directing us to what is crucially important in preaching, and that is the cross of Christ. The words "crucial" and "crux" both have their root in the Latin word for cross, *crux*, and they have come into the English language with their current meaning because the concept of the cross is at the very center and core of biblical Christianity. Paul is using hyperbole, a form of emphasis that uses intentional exaggeration. He declared many things regarding the revelation of God in Scripture, but in all of his preaching and in all of his missionary activity, the central point of importance was the cross. We are left in no doubt that the cross of Christ is the very hub of the Bible and the foundation on which the whole message of evangelism rests.

The Cross of Christ: Foretold in the Old Testament and the Gospels

There are scholars who claim that Paul preached a different gospel message from the Lord Jesus Christ. This is not so. We note what Paul has to say about his gospel in 1 Corinthians 15:3–7, beginning with these words: "For I delivered to you first of all that which I also received." Using terms equivalent to the technical rabbinic words for the reception and transmission of tradition, the apostle refers to the gospel as something that he had received and passed on. R. H. Mounce called this "without doubt the most valuable piece of pre-Pauline Christianity in the New Testament," and even "the oldest document of the Christian Church in existence."[1] The passage goes on: "that Christ died for our sins according to the Scriptures." In this the apostle Paul is setting forth with clarity the message of primitive Christianity.

It is significant that he adds "according to the Scriptures." The message was not something invented by the apostles. The message of the coming

---

1. R. H. Mounce as quoted in John Stott, *The Preacher's Portrait: Some New Testament Word Studies* (Grand Rapids: Eerdmans, 1961), 41.

death of the Messiah was prophesied throughout the period of the Old Testament. The first hint of it is given in the promise in Genesis 3:15:

> "And I will put enmity
> Between you and the woman,
> And between your seed and her Seed;
> He shall bruise your head,
> And you shall bruise His heel."

After the fall of our first parents and their expulsion from the garden of Eden, the problem became how a sinful creature can approach a holy God. Having incurred death as a result of disobedience, the only remedy lay in the punishment of death being taken by a substitute. This way of deliverance was signified in the offering of the Passover lamb in Egypt (Exodus 12). The Passover concept was continued in the Levitical sacrificial system by the recurring assurance that the sacrifices are made in order that the worshiper may be accepted before the Lord (Lev. 1:3–4).

The clearest revelation of the promised deliverer is found in the Servant Songs in the book of Isaiah. J. A. Motyer says, "The full Old Testament development of the principle of substitution came through the towering genius of Isaiah who saw that in ultimate reality, only a Person can substitute for persons."[2] Isaiah 53:5–6 offers a clear prediction of the vicarious sufferings of the Servant of the Lord:

> He was wounded for our transgressions,
> He was bruised for our iniquities;
> The chastisement of our peace was upon Him;
> And by His stripes we are healed....
> The LORD has laid on Him the iniquity of us all.

The Lord Jesus Christ identified with the Servant and saw His mission as coming "to give His life a ransom for many" (Mark 10:45) and to be "numbered with the transgressors" (Luke 22:37).

The sufferings and death of the Messiah are central in the structure of all four Gospels. They have been well described as passion narratives with extended introductions. In each gospel the death and resurrection take up what might be considered a disproportionate space. Of the eighty-nine

---

2. J. A. Motyer, *Look to the Rock: An Old Testament Background to Our Understanding of Christ* (Leicester: Inter-Varsity, 1996), 14.

chapters in the Gospels, twenty-five are given to what is known as the Passion Week. Everything is unfolding with a view to the climax in the suffering and death on the cross. As Jesus's supreme task, suffering and death were clearly present in His mind from the beginning of His public ministry. In accepting John's baptism, He identified Himself with sinners (Matt. 3:13–15). As soon as the disciples openly confessed Him as Messiah, He began to indicate to them that He must suffer and die (Matt. 16:21). Later on we are told, "He steadfastly set His face to go to Jerusalem" (Luke 9:51), and on the eve of His entry to Jerusalem He said, "The hour has come that the Son of Man should be glorified" (John 12:23). In His teaching Jesus clearly laid the foundation for a theology of the cross.

The Cross of Christ: The Theme of Apostolic Preaching

After the resurrection and ascension of the Lord Jesus Christ, His disciples waited in Jerusalem for the coming of the promised Holy Spirit. This was fulfilled on the day of Pentecost. What a transformation the event brought about in their thinking! In his Farewell Discourse to His disciples (John 14–16), the Lord Jesus Christ had promised that when the Holy Spirit came He would "teach you all things, and bring to your remembrance all things that I said to you" (John 14:26). When Peter preached on the day of Pentecost, he introduced his message with these words: "But this is what was spoken by the prophet Joel" (Acts 2:16).

What his hearers had witnessed was foretold by Joel in the Old Testament. The prophecies were concerned with the coming of Jesus of Nazareth (Acts 2:22), and Peter goes on to tell the facts of Christ's life and death; "Him, being delivered by the determined purpose and foreknowledge of God, you have taken by lawless hands, have crucified, and put to death; whom God raised up, having loosed the pains of death, because it was not possible that He should be held by it" (vv. 23–24). His message consisted of an account of something of great significance that had happened—and that was history. Then he went on to give the meaning of what was set forth: "Therefore let all the house of Israel know assuredly that God has made this Jesus, whom you crucified, both Lord and Christ." That was doctrine. As J. Gresham Machen pointed out: "Christ died—that is history; Christ died for our sins—that is doctrine. Without these two elements joined in an absolutely indissoluble union, there is no Christianity."[3] It is clear from the preaching in the Acts of the Apostles and in the teaching of the Epistles that the gospel to be heralded forth consists of four main elements, as summarized by J. I. Packer:

1. That all men are sinners and can do nothing to save themselves

2. That Jesus Christ, God's Son, is a perfect Savior for sinners, even the worst

3. That the Father and the Son have promised that all who know themselves to be sinners and put faith in Christ as Savior shall be received into favor and none cast out

4. That God has made repentance and faith a duty requiring of every man who hears the gospel "a serious full recumbency and rolling of the soul upon Christ in the promise of the gospel as an all-sufficient Savior, able to deliver and save to the utmost them that come to God by him; ready, able and willing, through the sufficiency of his ransom, to save every soul that shall freely give up themselves unto him for that end."[4]

In the light of the apostolic example we can surely concur with Packer, who comments, "The preacher's task...is to *display Christ*, to explain man's need of Him, His sufficiency to save, and His offer of Himself in the promises as Saviour to all who truly turn to Him."[5] The knowledge that is saving, according to Jonathan Edwards, is when the sinner has "a real sense of the excellency of God and Jesus Christ, of the work of redemption, and the ways and works of God revealed in the gospel."[6]

The Message That Ascribes All Glory to God

If we are to have a true understanding of God's revelation in creation and in redemption, we must consider that God's grand design is to glorify Himself and to show to the whole universe what an infinitely glorious being He is. Before the creation of the universe, the glory resided in the Trinity from all

---

3. J. Gresham Machen, *Christianity and Liberalism* (Grand Rapids: Eerdmans, 1923), 27.
4. J. I. Packer, introductory essay to *The Death of Death in the Death of Christ*, by John Owen (repr., London: Banner of Truth, 1959), 16.
5. Packer, introductory essay, 16.
6. Jonathan Edwards, "A Divine and Supernatural Light," in *The Works of President Edwards* (New York: Leavitt and Allen, 1852), 4:441.

eternity. Then there was a shining forth of that glory in the creation of the world and in man as the crown of that creation. Adam and Eve, created in the image of God, were able to behold the glory of God, to rejoice in that glory and to reflect it. As a result of the fall, man lost not only communion with God but also the image of God by which he beheld the glory of God at the first creation. But in the counsels of eternity, the triune God purposed and planned to restore the glory through the work of redemption.

The new manifestation of that glory came gradually. Prior to the revelation of the covenant of grace in redemptive history, we read that "the God of glory appeared to our father Abraham" (Acts 7:2). The glory that was manifested from time to time in the Old Testament was predicted to appear in a person. The call in Isaiah 40:3, 5, "Prepare the way of the LORD; make straight in the desert a highway for our God," goes on to declare, "The glory of the LORD shall be revealed, and all flesh shall see it together." That glory came in the person of the Messiah. As the baby lay in the manger, "the glory of the Lord shone around" the shepherds watching their flocks near Bethlehem (Luke 2:9). In his gospel John encapsulates the truth: "And the Word became flesh and dwelt among us, and we beheld His glory, the glory as of the only begotten of the Father, full of grace and truth" (John 1:14). "No one has seen God at any time. The only begotten Son, who is in the bosom of the Father, He has declared Him" (John 1:18). The original word for "declared" is the root from which we derive our word "exegesis." He gives us the truth about God. We can have confidence that the Father is as Christ declared Him to be.

Christ gives us not only the truth about the Father but He also reveals the grace of the triune God. The very coming of Christ in His incarnation, life, death, resurrection, and ascension makes known to the world what a God of love has done for the deliverance of hell-deserving sinners. God appears in human flesh with the purpose of reconciling the world unto Himself. Shortly before the time of the crucifixion, Christ said in prayer to His Father: "I have glorified You on the earth. I have finished the work which You have given Me to do" (John 17:4). The apex of His glory is the splendor of His grace. The revelation of the glory of God's grace was planned before creation and came to its climax in the death of Christ on the cross. This is the fullest revelation of the glory of God. The revelation in creation is glorious, but much more so the glory in redemption. Here we have the holiness, justice, and righteousness of God displayed in combination with His goodness, love, and mercy. It is a magnificent display of the attributes of God (Ps. 85:10–11).

We preach the doctrine of Christ crucified because it is the only place where sinners can behold the true glory of God. For that reason Satan, as "the god of this age," has blinded the minds of unbelievers, "lest the light of the gospel of the glory of Christ, who is the image of God, should shine on them" (2 Cor. 4:4). It therefore requires a supernatural work of God to counter the operation of Satan. This "divine and supernatural light," according to Jonathan Edwards, is the only remedy for the blindness: "For it is the God who commanded light to shine out of darkness, who has shone in our hearts to give the light of the knowledge of the glory of God in the face of Jesus Christ" (2 Cor. 4:6). This supernatural work of God ensures not only that we behold the glory of God in Christ but that all the glory is given to the triune God in the application of salvation. He has ordained that no flesh should glory in His presence.

Because the doctrine of the cross of Christ gives all the glory to God and humbles man in the dust, it is an offense to the natural man. This is why there are so many opposed to the truth who wish to reject it or to tone it down. It was a stumbling block to the Jews and foolishness to the Greeks (1 Cor. 1:23). To avoid such offense, the Judaizers in the churches of Galatia sought to add something to the cross (Gal. 6:12). Paul had to defend the true gospel against a "different gospel, which is not another." He boldly asserted, "But even if we, or an angel from heaven, preach any other gospel to you than what we have preached to you, let him be accursed" (Gal. 1:6–8). The false teachers were bringing outward ceremonies and works into the equation and telling the believers in Galatia what they should do. This salvation by good works and self-effort has been the religion of the natural man down through the centuries. In *Christianity and Liberalism*, J. Gresham Machen highlights the contrast between the two religions. Liberalism begins by telling the sinner what he must do; Christianity begins by telling the sinner what God has done. The liberal teacher offers us exhortation. The Christian evangelist offers not exhortation but a gospel.[7]

Another form of that self-reliant effort that detracts from the glory of the cross is Arminianism. It reared its head in the wake of the Reformation through the Dutch theologian James Arminius (1560–1609). Its central feature was an assertion of human moral ability to cooperate savingly with God's grace. A national synod was called at Dordrecht (1618–1619) which produced a response that came to be known as the five points of Calvinism.

---

7. Machen, *Christianity and Liberalism*, 47.

This defense safeguarded the supernatural nature of the grace of God by asserting total depravity, unconditional election, limited atonement, irresistible grace, and perseverance of the saints.

Packer sets out the importance of this:

> It cannot be over-emphasised that we have not seen the full meaning of the cross till we have seen it as the divines of Dort display it—as the centre of the Gospel, flanked on the one hand by total inability and unconditional election and on the other by irresistible grace and final preservation. For the full meaning of the cross only appears when the atonement is defined in terms of these four truths. Christ died to save a certain company of helpless sinners upon whom God has set His free saving love. Christ's death ensured the calling and keeping—the present and final salvation—of all whose sins he bore.[8]

The Powerfully Effective Message

Another reason why the preaching of the cross is foundational is because it produces the only power that can change human nature and work effectively in transforming society. Paul boasted in the cross and declared to the Christians in Rome: "For I am not ashamed of the gospel of Christ, for it is the power of God to salvation for everyone who believes, for the Jew first and also for the Greek" (Rom. 1:16).

The suitability of the gospel to the sinner's need is well presented by Samuel Davies:

> A religion for sinners must reveal a method of salvation for the lost, of pardon for the guilty, and of sanctifying grace for the weak and wicked. And, blessed be God! the gospel answers this end; and it is its peculiar excellency that it does so.... It is its glorious peculiarity that it reveals a method of salvation every way honourable to God and his government, and every way suitable to our necessities; and that is by the sufferings of Christ, the Founder of this religion. This is the ground, the substance, and marrow of the gospel; and it is this above all other things, that its ministers ought to preach and inculcate. It should have the same place in their sermons which it has in that gospel which it is their business to

---

8. Packer, introductory essay, 15.

preach; that is, it should be the foundation, the substance, the centre, the drift of all.[9]

Machen points out how the weak, discouraged disciples of Christ at the time of the crucifixion in a few days instituted the most powerful spiritual movement the world has ever seen:

> What had produced the astonishing change? What had transformed the weak and cowardly disciples into the spiritual conquerors of the world? Evidently it was not the mere memory of Jesus' life, for that was a source of sadness rather than of joy.... The great weapon with which the disciples of Christ set out to conquer the world was not a mere comprehension of eternal principles; it was an historical message, an account of something that had recently happened, it was the message, "He is risen."
> But the message of the resurrection was not isolated. It was connected with the death of Jesus, seen now to be not a failure, but a triumphant act of divine grace; it was connected with the entire appearance of Jesus upon earth.[10]

We find examples of the effect of preaching the cross of Christ in the experience of God's servants down through history. We discover that the great Scottish churchman Thomas Chalmers (1780–1847) spent the early years of his ministry at Kilmany in Fife thundering against the iniquities of Napoleon and grosser sorts of sins, but then when he was called from that congregation to Glasgow he said to his parishioners:

> For the first eight years of my twelve with you I thundered away against crimes of every sort, but the interesting fact is that during the whole of that period I never once heard of any reformation being urged upon you that I ever heard of those subordinate reformations which I made the ultimate object of my earlier ministry. You have taught me that to preach Jesus Christ is the only way of preaching morality, and the lesson I have learned in your humble cottages I shall carry into a wider field.[11]

We have in the life of Dr. D. Martyn Lloyd-Jones another example that illustrates the vital importance of the centrality of the cross in preaching.

---

9. "The Preaching of Christ Crucified as the Mean of Salvation," in *Sermons of the Rev. Samuel Davies* (repr., Pittsburgh: Soli Deo Gloria, 1993), 1:620–21.

10. Machen, *Christianity and Liberalism*, 28.

11. As quoted in Sidney Waterbury Powell, *Toward the Great Awakening* (New York: Abingdon-Cokesbury Press, 1949), 153.

He confided in several friends that a fundamental change took place on his outlook and preaching in the year 1929. He had emphasized from the beginning of his ministry the indispensable necessity of the new birth. But after preaching one night in Bridgend, South Wales, the minister challenged him that "the cross and the work of Christ" appeared to have little place in his preaching. Lloyd-Jones went to a secondhand bookseller and asked the proprietor for the two standard books on the atonement. He gave him R. W. Dale's *The Atonement* (1875) and James Denney's *The Death of Christ* (1903). On his return home he gave himself to study, declining both lunch and tea and causing his wife such anxiety that she telephoned her brother to see if a doctor should be called. But when he later emerged, he claimed to have found "the real heart of the gospel and the key to the inner meaning of the Christian faith." So the content of his preaching changed, and with this its impact. As he himself put it, the basic question was not that of Anselm—Why did God become man?—but, Why did Christ die?[12]

The Urgent Need of the Present Day

When we look at the declension that took place in the church in Britain in the second half of the nineteenth century, we can trace it to the inroads of higher criticism in universities and colleges and the spread of liberal theology. The uniqueness of the person and work of Christ was set aside, and He was understood not as the One who acts on our behalf to save us but the One who provides us with an example to follow. There were leaders within the church who saw the danger of this teaching and warned against it. One such leader was the well-known Scottish preacher and leader Horatius Bonar. In addressing the Free Church of Scotland General Assembly in 1883 he declared:

> No unsacrificial cross can pacify the conscience. No semi-sacrificial victim or quasi-substitutional propitiation will accomplish reconciliation and bid fear depart, bringing God and man together in righteous relationship never to be broken. The idealists of our time ask for a scientific cross; but there shall no such cross be given. Our philosophers call for a philosophical gospel; but there shall no such gospel be sent down from heaven. Our advanced thinkers and men of expansion demand a Christ for the nineteenth century; but no such Christ has arisen or shall

---

12. Iain H. Murray, *Martyn Lloyd-Jones: The First Forty Years* (Edinburgh: Banner of Truth, 1982), 1:190–91. See also John Stott, *The Cross of Christ* (Leicester: Inter-Varsity, 1986), 9.

arise. It must either be the first-century cross, the first-century gospel, the first-century Christ or no cross, no gospel, no Christ at all.[13]

The consequences of liberal theology were devastating for the church in Britain and later on for churches in other Western countries. The general trend was summed up in the well-known words from H. Richard Niebuhr: "A God without wrath brought men without sin into a Kingdom without judgment through the ministrations of a Christ without a cross."[14]

Even in the churches that retained the preaching of the cross there was a slide into the old Arminian teaching. In Britain during the 1950s mass evangelism was popular, but the type of gospel it communicated aroused questions. At the same time there was a recovery of the doctrines of grace, and minds were being directed to the writings of the Reformers and Puritans and the gospel prevalent in them. Among those who made a comparison was Dr. J. I. Packer. In his introductory essay to the reprint of John Owens's *Death of Death in the Death of Christ*, he wrote:

> The new gospel conspicuously fails to produce deep reverence, deep repentance, deep humility, a spirit of worship, a concern for the church. Why? We would suggest that the reason lies in its own character and content. It fails to make men God-centred in their thoughts and God-fearing in their hearts because that is not primarily what it is trying to do. One way of stating the difference between it and the old gospel is to say that it is exclusively concerned to be "helpful" to man—to bring peace, comfort, happiness, satisfaction—and too little concerned to glorify God.[15]

The crying need of today is to return to the cross-centered preaching of the Reformers, Puritans, and their successors. "Young man," said veteran Richard Sibbes to Thomas Goodwin, "if ever you would do good you must preach of the free grace of God in Christ Jesus." As Packer remarks, "The Puritans knew that the traveller through the Bible landscape loses his way as soon as he loses sight of the hill called Calvary."[16] In a later age the Southern

---

13. Horatius Bonar, *Our Ministry: How It Touches the Questions of the Age* (Edinburgh, 1883), 112.

14. H. Richard Niebuhr, *The Kingdom of God in America* (New York: Harper and Row, 1938), 193.

15. Packer, introductory essay, 1.

16. J. I. Packer, *A Quest for Godliness: The Puritan Vision of the Christian Life* (Wheaton, Ill.: Crossway, 1990), 286.

Presbyterian preacher Daniel Baker (1791–1857) spoke of the reason for the remarkable blessing that attended his ministry: "I was a man of one book, and that book the Bible: and taking the hint from an inspired Apostle, I made Jesus Christ and him crucified my constant theme." Writing to one of his sons, a young minister, he exhorted him:

> Remember, my son, this saying of your father, that the sermon that does not distinctly present Christ in the beauty and glory of his mediatorial character is no better than a cloud without water, a casket without a jewel, a shadow without the substance, or the body without the soul.[17]

17. As quoted in David B. Calhoun, *"Our Southern Zion": Old Columbia Seminary* (Edinburgh: Banner of Truth, 2012), 24.

CHAPTER 10

The Power of Preaching:
The Presence of the Holy Spirit

Michael A. G. Haykin

Andrew Fuller (1754–1815) is remembered for many things: his defense of the free offer of the gospel and his missional theology; his ardent affirmation of classical Christianity and keen rebuttal of major theological errors (like Deism and Socinianism) thrown up in the wake of the British Enlightenment; the key role that he played as the secretary of the fledgling Baptist Missionary Society from 1793 until his death in 1815; and his remarkable ability for sustaining vital Christian friendships with men like William Carey (1761–1834).[1] Preaching, though, is not something for which he is usually remembered.[2] Yet after his official call to the pastoral ministry of Soham Baptist Church in 1775 at the age of twenty-one, there were few Sundays that he did not preach between then and his death forty years later. Possibly one reason why he is often overlooked in surveys of the history of preaching is that, according to his early biographer and one-time friend, John Webster Morris (1763–1836),

---

1. For Fuller's life and ministry, see especially Peter J. Morden, *The Life and Thought of Andrew Fuller (1754–1815)* (Milton Keynes, England: Paternoster, 2015). For a briefer study, see Gilbert S. Laws, *Andrew Fuller: Pastor, Theologian, Ropeholder* (London: Carey Press, 1942). Also see the excellent study of "Fullerism" by E. F. Clipsham: "Andrew Fuller and Fullerism: A Study in Evangelical Calvinism," *The Baptist Quarterly* 20 (1963–1964): 99–114, 146–54, 214–25, 268–76.

2. There are a few studies of his preaching: see Edwin Charles Dargan, *A History of Preaching* (New York: Hodder & Stoughton/George H. Doran Co., 1912), 2:332–33; Harlice E. Keown, "The Preaching of Andrew Fuller" (ThM thesis, Southern Baptist Theological Seminary, 1957); Thomas R. McKibbens Jr., *The Forgotten Heritage: A Lineage of Great Baptist Preaching* (Macon, Ga.: Mercer University Press, 1986), 44–52; Paul Brewster, *Andrew Fuller: Model Pastor-Theologian* (Nashville: B&H Publishing, 2010), 110–20; Keith S. Grant, "Plain, Evangelical, and Affectionate: The Preaching of Andrew Fuller (1754–1815)," *Crux* 48, no.1 (Spring 2012): 12–22; Keith S. Grant, *Andrew Fuller and the Evangelical Renewal of Pastoral Theology* (Eugene, Ore.: Wipf & Stock, 2013), 77–104.

[Fuller] had none of that easy elocution, none of that graceful fluency, which melts upon the ear, and captivates the attention of an auditor. His enunciation was laborious and slow; his voice strong and heavy; occasionally plaintive, and capable of an agreeable modulation. He had none of that eloquence which consists in a felicitous selection of terms, or in the harmonious construction of periods; he had a boldness in his manner, a masculine delivery, and great force of expression.[3]

And yet, as Morris admitted, Fuller turned out to be a popular preacher; by the close of his ministry, a thousand or so would regularly attend his preaching in Kettering.[4] More positively, Morris did note that Fuller's "preaching was distinguished for depth of thought, a fulness of scriptural truth, and great perspicacity and force.... It was like a blazing torch in the midst of the churches."[5] Fuller also preached in a day when there were a number of pulpit celebrities, including his friend the inimitable Robert Hall Jr. (1764–1831),[6] the memory of whose preaching overshadowed that of many others, including Fuller.

Whatever the reasons for the "forgotten heritage" of Fuller's sermonic corpus,[7] it is evident from various sources, including a large number of extant ordination sermons, that Fuller gave much thought to the significance and nature of preaching in pastoral ministry. The following paper, written in celebration of the powerful pulpit ministry of my dear friend Dr. Steve Lawson, seeks to isolate one aspect of Fuller's thinking about preaching as necessary in his day as it is in ours: divine unction.

---

3. John Webster Morris, *Memoirs of the Life and Writings of the Rev. Andrew Fuller* (London, 1816), 66–67.

4. Morris, *Memoirs*, 66, 79.

5. Morris, *Memoirs*, 82–83. A younger contemporary, Francis Augustus Cox (1783–1853), similarly recalled Fuller as "an extraordinary preacher: plain, practical, judicious, full of rich scriptural illustrations," though "slow and solemn" in his manner of preaching (as cited in Andrew Gunton Fuller, "Memoir," in *The Complete Works of the Rev. Andrew Fuller*, ed. Joseph Belcher [1845; repr., Harrisonburg, Va.: Sprinkle Publications, 1988], 1:105–7, note *).

6. See the brief discussion of Hall's preaching by McKibbens Jr., *Forgotten Heritage*, 61–66, and the larger study by Cody Heath McNutt, "The Ministry of Robert Hall, Jr.: The Preacher as Theological Exemplar and Cultural Celebrity" (PhD diss., The Southern Baptist Theological Seminary, 2012).

7. The phrase is from the title of McKibbens Jr. in *Forgotten Heritage*.

"Full of the Holy Spirit"

Thomas R. McKibbens Jr., author of *The Forgotten Heritage: A Lineage of Great Baptist Preaching*, finds Fuller's thinking about the task of the preacher, which he expressed in a letter to his friend John Ryland Jr. (1753–1825), to be a helpful summary. Fuller wrote about the students under Ryland's care at Bristol Baptist Academy, where Ryland had been the principal since 1793: "I wish they may so believe and feel and preach the truth, as to find their message an important reality, influencing their own souls and the souls of others."[8] If the preacher's life and the lives of his hearers are to be shaped by the "important reality" of the Scriptures, he needs to "believe and feel" the truth he preaches. But where does this power to "believe and feel" come from? For Fuller, it was incontestable that there is only one source, namely, the indispensable presence of the Holy Spirit.

Fuller's lengthiest discussion of this element of preaching is found in one of his earliest ordination sermons. Based on Acts 11:24, it was preached at the ordination of Robert Fawkner on October 31, 1787, in Thorn, Bedfordshire.[9] The context of this verse in Acts is the ministry of Barnabas at Antioch. The

---

8. *The Last Remains of the Rev. Andrew Fuller*, ed. Joseph Belcher (Philadelphia, Pa.: American Baptist Publication Society, [1856]), 358. For similar remarks by Fuller, see his "Spiritual Knowledge and Love Necessary for the Ministry," in *Complete Works of the Rev. Andrew Fuller*, 1:480–81; "The Nature of the Gospel, and Manner in Which It Ought to Be Preached," in *Complete Works of the Rev. Andrew Fuller*, 1:496; "Habitual Devotedness to the Ministry," in *Complete Works of the Rev. Andrew Fuller*, 1:507; and "Affectionate Concern of a Minister for the Salvation of His Hearers," in *Complete Works of the Rev. Andrew Fuller*, 1:508.

9. "The Qualifications and Encouragement of a Faithful Minister Illustrated by the Character and Success of Barnabas," in *Complete Works of the Rev. Andrew Fuller*, 1:135–44. This sermon was initially published in 1787 along with John Ryland's charge to the church at Thorn: *The Qualifications and Encouragement of a Faithful Minister, Illustrated by the Character and Success of Barnabas; and, Paul's Charge to the Corinthians Respecting Their Treatment of Timothy, Applied to the Conduct of Churches toward Their Pastors* (London: For Thorn Baptist Church, 1787). The sermon was reprinted in America at the beginning of the nineteenth century in a booklet with two other sermons by Fuller and was titled *Three Occasional Sermons* (Boston, Mass.: Manning & Loring, 1801). This booklet was reprinted again in 1809 as an appendix to Fuller's *Memoirs of the Late Rev. Samuel Pearce, A.M.* (Newark, N.J.: E. B. Gould, 1809), 57–78.

For the early history of the church at Thorn to the close of Fawkner's pastorate in 1794, see [Charles E. Duffy,] *Houghton Regis Baptist Church* (Dunstable, Bedfordshire: Miles Taylor, 1925), 2–4. Fuller maintained contact with the Thorn church after this ordination sermon. Thus, when a daughter work was planted in nearby Houghton Regis, Fuller was asked to preach at this congregation's first service early in 1804. He preached on 1 Samuel 5:8 ([Duffy,] *Houghton Regis Baptist Church*, 5). See also the details about the Thorn and Houghton Regis congregations in Scott Wilson, "A5/M1 Link Road: Thorn Farm Burial Ground

verse describes Barnabas as "a good man, full of the Holy Spirit and of faith," and then adds after this description, "and a great many people were added to the Lord."

In his sermon Fuller first explained the implications of the description of Barnabas as a "good man." He then turned to the phrase "full of the Holy Spirit." Fuller understood this to mean that Barnabas was "full of those fruits of the Spirit mentioned" in Galatians 5:22–23 and was, as it were, "overcome…with the holy influences and fruits of the blessed Spirit." A pastor, in other words, must be a man whose inner life is being deeply shaped by the transformative work of the Holy Spirit. Fuller equated this to what is described in 1 John 2:20 as "an anointing from the Holy One" and observed that such an anointing was vital for pastoral ministry.[10]

In Fuller's mind, there were five ways in which this unction shapes a pastor's life. First, it enables the pastor "to enter into the spirit of the gospel" and to rightly understand the truths at the heart of the Christian faith. In fact, Fuller was convinced that if Christians in general "had more of the Holy Spirit of God in their hearts" there would be far less friction between them concerning such great truths as "the loveliness of the Divine character," "the exceeding sinfulness of sin, the total depravity of mankind, the proper Deity and atonement of Christ, justification by faith in his name, the freeness and sovereignty of grace, and the agency of the Holy Spirit."[11] All of these truths had come into dispute in eighteenth-century England as a result of the rationalism of the British Enlightenment, and, Fuller implied, only the Holy Spirit's presence could protect the pastor against speculations aroused by this corrosive rationalism.[12] Little wonder he urged Fawkner to make Psalm 51:11 his prayer: "Do not take Your Holy Spirit from me."[13]

Historical Research," Persona Associates, accessed September 28, 2015, http://www.persona .uk.com/A5dunstable/deposit-docs/DD101-DD125/DD-112.pdf.

10. "Qualifications and Encouragement of a Faithful Minister," in *Complete Works of the Rev. Andrew Fuller*, 1:135, 138–39.

11. "Qualifications and Encouragement of a Faithful Minister," in *Complete Works of the Rev. Andrew Fuller*, 1:139.

12. See also "Churches Walking in the Truth, the Joy of Ministers," in *Complete Works of the Rev. Andrew Fuller*, 1:530; "Faith in the Gospel a Necessary Prerequisite to Preaching It," in *Complete Works of the Rev. Andrew Fuller*, 1:516. This latter address was preached to the students at Bristol Baptist Academy.

13. "Qualifications and Encouragement of a Faithful Minister," in *Complete Works of the Rev. Andrew Fuller*, 1:139.

Second, Fuller was convinced that "being full of the Holy Spirit" will lead a preacher to use the very words of Holy Scripture that the Holy Spirit has inspired rather than various alternatives which, while they might be more familiar to the ears of the preacher's audience, nonetheless subtly change the meaning of what is being communicated. Examples of such sermonic substitutions from his own day, according to Fuller, were to use "morality" in place of "holiness," "virtue" instead of "godliness," "good men" for "believers [and] saints," or to replace "communion with God" with "happiness of mind." If such substitutions become the norm, Fuller reasoned, it would result in "the gospel heathenized, and will tend to heathenize the minds" of both the preacher and hearer. For Fuller, the Spirit's help is not only vital in the discernment of biblical truth but also in its communication: "Spiritual things will be spiritually discerned, and if spiritually discerned, will be spiritually communicated." The anointing of the Holy Spirit will thus give a man a desire to speak in the language used by the Holy Spirit in the Scriptures. As Fuller told Fawkner: The more you are filled with "an unction from the Holy One, the greater relish you will possess for that savoury manner of conveying truth" as found in terms drawn directly from the Bible.[14] Fuller's use of affective terms here—"relish," "savoury"—is noteworthy. It is obvious that, for Fuller, the infilling of the Holy Spirit is closely tied to the creation of a spiritual appetite.

Third, the Spirit's anointing, then, will be seen in a harmony between what a man preaches and inculcates from the pulpit and how he lives his life, for, and here Fuller cited Proverbs 17:7 as proof, "Excellent speech becometh not a fool."[15] Fourth, this anointing will "give a spiritual savour" to the minister's speech as he visits the members of his church and enables him to love them.[16] Finally, the Spirit's infilling will impart to the minister "a meek, mild, peaceful, humble spirit." It is noteworthy that these final three effects of the Spirit's anointing concern more than simply the act of sermon preparation

---

14. "Qualifications and Encouragement of a Faithful Minister," in *Complete Works of the Rev. Andrew Fuller*, 1:140. See also "On an Intimate and Practical Acquaintance with the Word of God," in *Complete Works of the Rev. Andrew Fuller*, 1:484; "The Satisfaction Derived from Godly Simplicity," in *Complete Works of the Rev. Andrew Fuller*, 1:540–41; *Strictures on Some of the Leading Sentiments of Mr. R. Robinson*, in *Complete Work of the Rev. Andrew Fuller*, 3:609: "I must confess, I am…attached to Scripture phraseology."

15. "Qualifications and Encouragement of a Faithful Minister," in *Complete Works of the Rev. Andrew Fuller*, 1:140.

16. "Qualifications and Encouragement of a Faithful Minister," in *Complete Works of the Rev. Andrew Fuller*, 1:140–41.

and its delivery. The unction of the Spirit, in Fuller's thinking, does not simply relate to empowerment in preaching but has an effect upon the preacher's entire life and ministry.

"Eminent Spirituality in a Minister"

After he explained what it meant for Barnabas to be "full of faith," Fuller closed Fawkner's ordination sermon with a discussion of the final phrase of Acts 11:24, "and a great many people were added to the Lord." He discerned that Luke's placement of this phrase immediately after his description of Barnabas was intended to lead the reader to draw a connection between Barnabas's character and his success as a minister. Fuller was unwilling to argue that ministerial success is automatically dependent upon spirituality. In other words, he was convinced, as was most of Western Christianity after the fourth-century Donatist controversy, that "the quality and state of he who administers the sacraments and the Word of God...did not have an influence on its efficacy."[17] Nevertheless, Fuller did believe that ministerial "want of usefulness is often to be ascribed to...want of spirituality, much oftener than to...want of talents." He thus laid it down as a rule: "Eminent spirituality in a minister is usually attended with eminent usefulness," where "eminent spirituality" is to be understood in light of what Fuller has already said about the fullness of the Holy Spirit, or the Holy Spirit's anointing.[18]

Such eminent spirituality is manifest in three ways. First, it is characterized by a "holy love to Christ and the souls of men." For illustration, Fuller turned to three examples from the Old Testament—Hezekiah, Ezra, and Nehemiah. He knew of many other notable examples, but he was running short on time, so he had to say:

> Time would fail me to speak of all the great souls, both inspired and uninspired, whom the King of kings has delighted to honour: of Paul, and Peter, and their companions; of [John] Wickliff, and [Martin] Luther, and [John] Calvin, and many others at the Reformation; of [John] Elliot, and [Jonathan] Edwards, and [David] Brainerd, and [George] Whitefield, and hundreds more whose names are held in deserved esteem in

17. Alexander Bitzel, "The Theology of the Sermon in the Eighteenth Century," trans. Charlotte Masemann, in *Preaching, Sermon and Cultural Change in the Long Eighteenth Century*, ed. Joris van Eijnatten (Leiden: Brill, 2009), 64.

18. "Qualifications and Encouragement of a Faithful Minister," in *Complete Works of the Rev. Andrew Fuller*, 1:142–43.

the church of God. These were men of God; men who had great grace, as well as gifts; whose hearts burned in love to Christ and the souls of men. They looked upon their hearers as their Lord had done upon Jerusalem, and wept over them.[19]

This list of Fuller's heroes reflects his catholicity and willingness to look beyond his own Calvinistic Baptist heritage for models in ministry. And yet it bears noting that after the death of his close friend Samuel Pearce (1766–1799) of Birmingham, Fuller did not hesitate to recommend this Calvinistic Baptist pastor as a model preacher. As he stated in a later ordination sermon with regard to the way in which the gospel should be preached: "Consider the examples held up for your imitation. You have Peter…Paul…John…. Nay, more—you have Christ. Nor have you examples in distant ages only; but you have seen some, even among you…Pearce!"[20]

"Eminent spirituality" also produces an ardency for "the glory of God, and the welfare of men's souls," which are "ends which God himself pursues." As Fuller pithily observed in another ordination sermon, "a cold manner" in preaching "disgraces important truth."[21] Third, "eminent spirituality" is accompanied by a genuine humility. In fact, Fuller wondered if "one considerable reason why most of us have no more real success in our work than we have" is because "we have not grace enough to bear prosperity."[22]

"The Presence of Christ"

A second ordination sermon in which Fuller dealt with the spiritual anointing pastors need is a much smaller text and more typical of the sermons that survive, for Fuller rarely wrote out a full manuscript before preaching.[23]

---

19. "Qualifications and Encouragement of a Faithful Minister," in *Complete Works of the Rev. Andrew Fuller*, 1:143–44.

20. "Nature of the Gospel," in *Complete Works of the Rev. Andrew Fuller*, 1:496. See also "Spiritual Knowledge and Love Necessary for the Ministry," in *Complete Works of the Rev. Andrew Fuller*, 1:481; "Affectionate Concern of a Minister for the Salvation of His Hearers," in *Complete Works of the Rev. Andrew Fuller*, 1:508: "Look at the men who have been the most honoured; and you will find that they are not the brightest geniuses, but the humble and affectionate."

21. "Affectionate Concern of a Minister," in *Complete Works of the Rev. Andrew Fuller*, 1:510.

22. "Qualifications and Encouragement of a Faithful Minister," in *Complete Works of the Rev. Andrew Fuller*, 1:144.

23. See his comments about sermon manuscripts in *Thoughts on Preaching, in Letters to a Young Minister*, in *Complete Works of the Rev. Andrew Fuller*, 1:714.

Neither the date nor the context of this ordination sermon is known. Fuller's text on the occasion was the benediction of 2 Timothy 4:22, "The Lord Jesus Christ be with your spirit."[24] The blessing in view here, Fuller explained, is nothing less than "communion with Christ," the "unction by which we know all things" (an allusion to 1 John 2:20), and the source of grace in the life of any true pastor.[25]

Fuller delineated four implications of this blessing/communion/anointing—without which nothing can be done for Christ. First, it leads the minister to "delight in the doctrine of Christ." In other words, his preaching is solidly Christ centered. As Fuller noted about such preaching in another ordination sermon: "We preach 'Christ Jesus the Lord.' This is the grand theme of the Christian ministry.... Preach Christ, or you had better be any thing than a preacher.... If you preach Christ, you need not fear for want of matter. His person and work are rich in fullness."[26]

Then, this blessing "gives a divine energy to our preaching."[27] Such "energy," Fuller hastened to point out, is quite different from "the greatest eloquence," for the latter is never "a means of conversion" or conviction. Fuller found biblical evidence for this assertion in the preaching of Stephen (Acts 6:10), Apollos (Acts 18:25, 28), and Paul (1 Cor. 2:4), where the common factor is the empowerment of the Holy Spirit.[28]

Third, this anointing will make pastoral visitation "savoury and useful." Finally, this anointing is needed to withstand the various trials involved in pastoral ministry: the way that God's people grieve their leaders—Fuller does not say anything about church leaders grieving the congregation, though this also happens—and hurt each other; and the way that some of the church members reject their pastor's doctrinal views or criticize aspects of his mode

24. "The Influence of the Presence of Christ on a Minister," in *Complete Works of the Rev. Andrew Fuller*, 1:504–5.

25. "Influence of the Presence of Christ," in *Complete Works of the Rev. Andrew Fuller*, 1:504–5.

26. "Preaching Christ," in *Complete Works of the Rev. Andrew Fuller*, 1:503. Based on a reference at the outset of this sermon to Abraham Booth being deceased, it should be dated after 1806, the year of Booth's death ("Preaching Christ," in *Complete Works of the Rev. Andrew Fuller*, 1:501).

27. "Preaching Christ," in *Complete Works of the Rev. Andrew Fuller*, 1:505.

28. Fuller clearly understood the phrase "fervent in the spirit" (Acts 18:25 KJV) to be a reference to the Holy Spirit, not Apollos's own inner spirit.

of living.[29] Again, it is noteworthy that Fuller does not restrict the anointing of the Spirit to a sermonic context. It must accompany the Christian leader throughout the various areas of his life.

"Very Affecting" but Not "Enthusiastic"

In the judgment of Edwin Dargan, the early twentieth-century Southern Baptist historian of preaching, Fuller was "a strong expounder of the Scriptures," but his sermons contain "little warmth—no heat; imagination is scarcely in evidence at all; and 'flights of eloquence' nowhere appear."[30] Dargan, of course, never actually heard Fuller preach. George Wallis, a member of Fuller's congregation who regularly sat under his preaching, described it in his diary as "very affecting and evangelical."[31] Fuller himself actually decried preaching "without feeling," for, he asked, "How can we display the evil of sin, the love of Christ, or any other important truth, unless we feel it?" He could tell a newly ordained pastor that the "gospel is a message of love, and therefore it ought to be preached with great affection."[32] The preacher, both in his preparation to preach and the preaching itself, must pursue these tasks with genuine heartfelt and heartburning ardor.[33] The place where such ardor was kindled was in private prayer. "Walking with God in the closet," Fuller once noted in an ordination sermon on John 5:35, "is a grand means, with his blessing, of illuminating our minds and warming our hearts."[34] In these times of private prayer, Fuller presumably expected the minister to pray for, among other things, the anointing of the Spirit.

At the heart of Fuller's understanding of preaching, then, was that it must be grounded in ardent love—for God and for people—but like many others in the eighteenth century he was opposed to what that era called "enthusiasm"—that is, the assertion of spiritual affections without the Spirit-given means. For instance, Fuller emphasized that the anointing of the Spirit did

---

29. "Influence of the Presence of Christ," in *Complete Works of the Rev. Andrew Fuller*, 1:505.

30. Dargan, *History of Preaching*, 2:333.

31. As cited in Grant, "Plain, Evangelical, and Affectionate," 17.

32. "Nature of the Gospel," in *Complete Works of the Rev. Andrew Fuller*, 1:496.

33. "Spiritual Knowledge and Love Necessary," in *Complete Works of the Rev. Andrew Fuller*, 1:480–81.

34. "Spiritual Knowledge and Love Necessary," in *Complete Works of the Rev. Andrew Fuller*, 1:482. See also "Intimate and Practical Acquaintance," in *Complete Works of the Rev. Andrew Fuller*, 1:484: "Let all your private meditations be mingled with prayer."

not relieve the preacher of study. "It is a shameful abuse of the doctrine of Divine influence," he asserted, "to allege it as a reason for neglecting diligent study for the pulpit."[35] Spirituality and learning are not mutually exclusive. What Fuller prized was the commingling of both. He stated as much in an address he gave in the final years of his life to the students of what was then called the Baptist Academical Institution at Stepney in London, established in 1810:

> To what is it owing that some of our churches have been prejudiced against an educated ministry? I may be told, to their ignorance; and in part it is so; but in part it is owing to other causes. The lightness, the vanity, the foppery, and the irreligion of some young men have pro-duced not only this effect, but an abhorrence of the very worship of God, as by them administered. Who were ever known to be prejudiced against [Samuel] Pearce, a [Benjamin] Francis, or a [Benjamin] Bed-dome, on account of their education? If there were individuals of this description, let them be disregarded as ignorant, and let them be told that vicious characters are found among the uneducated as well as the educated. But be it your concern, my dear young men, to shun these evils. The instructions which you receive, if consecrated to Christ, will be a blessing to you; but if your object be to shine before men, they will be a curse.[36]

There were some in the English Baptist congregations of Fuller's day who were deeply suspicious of learning because they had encountered seminary students who were marked by "vanity…foppery, and…irreligion." But that was no reason to reject learning, Fuller argued. He then cited the examples of three remarkable eighteenth-century Baptists whom he had personally known—Samuel Pearce, Benjamin Francis (1734–1799) of Horsley, and Ben-jamin Beddome (1717–1795) of Bourton-on-the-Water—all three of whom were graduates of Bristol Baptist Academy, but all of whom were known for their preaching and piety.[37] Learning per se is no impediment to spiritual unction, as these three men clearly demonstrated.

35. "Habitual Devotedness to the Ministry," in *Complete Works of the Rev. Andrew Fuller*, 1:506.

36. "The Young Minister Exhorted to Make Full Proof of His Ministry," in *Complete Works of the Rev. Andrew Fuller*, 1:520.

37. On Pearce, see Michael A. G. Haykin and Jerry Slate, *Samuel Pearce* (unpublished manuscript, 2015); on Francis, see Michael A. G. Haykin, "The Fire of Ardent Love: The Life and Witness of Benjamin Francis (1734–1799)," *Reformation Today* 173 (Jan–Feb 2000):

Fuller himself did not have formal theological education, but that did not prevent him from using his God-given abilities to become a first-rate preacher of God's Word. As the nineteenth-century doyen of homiletics John A. Broadus noted: although "Andrew Fuller...had practically no knowledge of the original languages [of the Bible]...his interpretations of Scripture are clear and safe in a degree very rarely surpassed."[38] But, as we have seen in this chapter, there is another reason for the impact of Fuller's preaching—namely, what he had described in 1787 in the Thorn Baptist meetinghouse as "eminent spirituality."

5–14; and on Beddome, see Michael A. G. Haykin, "Benjamin Beddome (1717–1795): His Life and His Hymns," in *Pulpit and People: Studies in Eighteenth Century Baptist Life and Thought*, ed. John H. Y. Briggs (Milton Keynes, U.K.: Paternoster, 2009), 93–111.

38. John A. Broadus, *On the Preparation and Delivery of Sermons*, ed. Jesse Burton Weatherspoon, rev. ed. (New York: Harper Brothers, 1944), 29.

PART 4
The Method of Preaching

CHAPTER 11

Preparing the Sermon

Iain D. Campbell

My default position when asked how long it takes me to prepare a sermon is to say "a lifetime." That is not an original thought, but when I came across it first I realized that it contains more than a kernel of truth. Every sermon we prepare, craft, and preach has the accumulated experience and knowledge, reading, and learning of a lifetime poured into it.

In and of itself, of course, that does not guarantee that it will be a good sermon; but it is a reminder to us that if preaching is "truth through personality," our personalities are forged over years of experience, and we are never the same person in the pulpit as we were the last time we stood there. God, through His Providence, shapes the preachers who shape the sermons, and Providence has a way of ensuring that we are never the same preacher twice.

But what is always the same is the word we are preaching. God's revealed and inscripturated revelation is the truth which lasts from age to age, and truth is the preacher's constant companion in all his ages too. James W. Alexander was right, therefore, to suggest that "constant perusal and re-perusal of Scripture is the great preparation for preaching. You get good even when you know it not."[1]

In the matter of sermon preparation, however, perusing is not enough. There must be what Alec Motyer calls "analysis" of the text: the kind of study that "forces us to ponder detail," for, he adds, "in the detail lies the mind of God."[2] It is with the matter of studying the detail that this chapter is concerned, and I am grateful for the opportunity to honor my colleague and friend Steve Lawson in doing so.

---

1. James W. Alexander, *Thoughts on Preaching* (Edinburgh, 1864), 30.
2. Alec Motyer, *Preaching?: Simple Teaching on Simply Preaching* (Fearn, Ross-shire, Scotland: Christian Focus, 2013), 60.

Announcing the Word

Questions of methodology are meaningless, of course, unless we are clear about what it is we are doing: What is the end to which the preparation of the sermon is the means? What is preaching? And what is a sermon?

There are other contributions to this *Festschrift* that will give more detailed answers to these questions, but we need to be clear that a sermon has ultimately only one aim: to enable men and women to hear what God is saying in His Word. Preaching is, to use Calvin's language, "the ordinary mode which the Lord has appointed for conveying His Word."[3] The sermon has not done its work unless it has given God's Word room to shine in its own light.

We can nuance that further by saying that preaching is the act of the triune God by which His purposes of grace and salvation, which could otherwise never have been known, are announced publicly before men for His glory. In preaching—as in all that God does—the acts of the persons of the Godhead are indivisible. God the Father gives His words of life to His children (John 17:8). God the Son fulfills His mediatorial commission as God's final prophet (Matt. 17:5; Heb. 1:2) and sanctifies His people "with the washing of water by the word" (Eph. 5:26). God the Holy Spirit teaches His people by words that are spiritual (1 Cor. 2:13). In this context, preaching is elevated from being a mere art form in which we, as preachers, are trained and constrained to excel: properly speaking, the preaching of God's Word belongs to the realm of theology. As the Westminster Larger Catechism 154 puts it, the word, especially in its preached form, is an "outward means whereby Christ communicates to His church the benefits of His mediation."

But for those of us who are called to be preachers, there is an artistry to the phenomenon of preaching for which we require training and which we hone by experience. Not least of these is the skill of unpacking the great truths and doctrines of Scripture as we explicate and apply the biblical text in our sermons. For that to be possible, we must become expert in the use of words—in their meaning, nuance, force, and power. In the beginning was the Word, and words are all we have for the act of preaching.

That means, of course, that sermons may employ extrabiblical words and material for the purpose of explaining and opening up the Bible's own words and material. They often do, and must. Truth is indivisible, and the truth of the Word of God can be further elucidated by truth from outside of itself.

---

3. John Calvin, *Commentaries on the Epistle of Paul to the Romans*, vol. 19 of *Calvin's Commentaries* (Grand Rapids: Baker, 2009), 398 (on Rom. 10:14).

But it cannot be illuminated by what is not true or by what is unbiblical. The discipline of sermon preparation is the discipline of discerning what may helpfully and legitimately be employed by way of opening up a Bible passage.

But that means two things: it means interpreting the text, and it means applying the text. In his preface to his magisterial commentary on the Bible, the Puritan Matthew Henry wrote that he had only two questions to ask of any passage on which he was commenting: "We must…inquire not only *What is this?* but *What is this to us?*"[4] For, as Henry explains, "we are concerned not only to understand what we read, but to improve it to some good purpose."

That is also what the best preaching will do. It will help us understand what is being said to us by God, and it will help us live by it. It will open to us the meaning of Scripture and enable us to live by its rule. It will inform our mind and direct our will. Preaching means more than conveying the sum total of the meanings of the individual words in the passage before us; it means enabling both us and our hearers to understand the words so as then to live in the light of them. And, as Matthew Henry implies, that requires asking some basic questions of the text.

Ultimately, the aim of the sermon is to show us Jesus and, under the blessing of the Holy Spirit, either to convict us that we are unlike Him when we ought not to be or to confirm us in the endeavor of being as like Him as we ought to be. Christ washes us by means of the word (Eph. 5:26). He does not simply inform us.

That, says Paul, is the aim of his preaching too: to warn and instruct every man in order that He might present everyone perfect before God (Col. 1:28). The preaching of the Word—the sermon—terminates upon Jesus Himself.

Approaching the Word

The sermon, then, takes its beginning on the pages of the Bible. It has to be related organically and dynamically to the living, infallible, and inerrant text of Scripture. It finds its genesis in the special, concursive, historical revelation of God, which has been written down for us in the Bible and preserved for us through the ages. There is no authentic sermon that has not been birthed from within the contents of God's Holy Scripture.

The preacher's concern is with two sets of words, therefore: the words on the page that is before him, and the words of the sermon that comes from

---

4. Matthew Henry, preface to *An Exposition of the Old and New Testament* (London, 1811), 1:viii.

him. The concern of this chapter is with the primary task of rightly under-standing and interpreting the text: what belongs to the area of hermeneutics.

Of course, strictly speaking, the primary area of preparation is not in hermeneutics but in the preparation of the preacher himself. We heralds of the good news need to be holy vessels for conveying that news before we begin asking what the news to be conveyed is. We ought to pray for understanding and appropriation of the truth so that we will be grasped by the grandeur and glory of what we read, even as we pray that others will be transformed by the truth we preach. I warm to the truth conveyed in the minister's prayer, even if I have to repent at how far short I come of it:

> I myself need thy support, comfort, strength, holiness,
>   that I might be a pure channel of thy grace,
>   and be able to do something for thee;…
> Help me not to treat excellent matter in a defective way.…
> And keep me in tune with thee as I do this work.[5]

That being said, the preacher's first task in the preparation of a sermon is to understand the Bible. The Bible is not a manual of sermons. But it is the material of our sermons. We need to comprehend what we are reading before we can begin to help others understand it too. It is for this reason that we invest time and money in theological colleges and seminaries, in order to equip preachers to employ the tools required for exegesis and interpre-tation of biblical texts. I love the insight of question 103 of the Heidelberg Catechism that the fourth commandment requires "that the ministry of the gospel and the schools [the theological seminaries] be maintained." If we do not maintain the seminaries of the churches, how can we provide preachers who will enable the Lord's people to keep the Christian Sabbath? And if we do not make preaching the key of our Sabbath keeping, how will we or our people keep the other nine commandments during our working week?

For those whose calling it is to be regular and, especially, full-time preach-ers of the Word, these tools and techniques are constantly being relearned and honed. The skillful butcher buys a good set of knives as he embarks on his trade, but he knows that sometimes they need to be sharpened or even replaced with better ones. As creators and deliverers of sermons, we are in the business of finding the best tools for the best work.

---

5. "A Minister's Preaching," in *The Valley of Vision: A Collection of Puritan Prayers and Devotions*, ed. Arthur Bennett (Edinburgh: Banner of Truth, 2009), 349.

Appreciating the Word

To preach on any given occasion requires making a selection of the text on which the sermon will be based. I have already written on the relative merits and pitfalls of preaching sequentially through Bible books, on the one hand, and of preaching on isolated texts, on the other, and frequently encourage preachers not to be enslaved to any methodology.[6] I am more concerned that preachers go deep into the Bible's meaning than that they go wide over its surface. The choice of text will be determined by the different circumstances of the preacher's situation, but I think it is generally true that the more narrow the focus, the more concentrated will be the thought in the sermon itself.

So what do we do as we approach the words before us in the initial stages of sermon preparation? It seems to me that there are three fundamental principles for the analysis of the biblical text in this regard.

The Bible Is Contextualized Revelation

When it comes to language, context is king. If you don't agree, how do you know what the word "king" in the previous sentence means? All the words of Scripture are God breathed and God given (2 Tim. 3:16), and God sets them side by side with other words so that their meaning may be known to us. The Bible is not a lexicon, but a storybook in which there are many literary types. The words, the basic building blocks of literature, require to be understood, and only their context can help us understand them.

But the circles of context in the Bible are concentric. Like ripples in a pond, they are ever widening. First, the words of the text have an immediate context in the sentence or paragraph in which they are located. If we preach on part of John 17, for example, we have to recognize that the chapter is a wonderful unit of text, in which we eavesdrop on the Son speaking to His Father about Himself and His disciples, having just finished speaking to His disciples about Himself and His Father. The immediate context informs the meaning of the text and provides a solid ground where we may drop anchor for the sermon.

Second, the words of the text also have a canonical context. The words are located in chapters, and the chapter in a book. The chapter divisions are artificial, of course, but their artifice is still useful. The sweep of the book, on the other hand, will feed into the meaning of the particular passage within

---

6. Iain D. Campbell, *Pray, Plan, Prepare, Preach: Establishing and Maintaining Priorities in the Preaching Ministry* (Leominster, England: Day One Publications, 2012), 48–62.

it on which we are preaching. John, to continue our example, tells us that his gospel is a select record, not a complete biography of Jesus's life, and the selection is with a view to us believing that He is the Son of God so that we will have eternal life (John 20:31). That aim informs the meaning of the passage and the reason for it; in everything John writes there is a link both forward and backward to the stated purpose for which he does so. Similarly, the word "generations" in Genesis 2:4 in several Bible translations has a meaning which focuses our attention on the origin and development of the natural world, as each successive use of the word (for example, at 5:1; 10:1; and so on) draws us to consider blocks of history. But the repetition of the word is organically linked to the protevangelium of Genesis 3:15, where it is in the seed of the woman, across the generations of history, that salvation will come. Words create sentences, and sentences paragraphs, and paragraphs chapters, and the whole builds to become a canonical unit.

Third, we locate the words in their wider biblical context. We believe not only in the verbal inspiration of God's Word but also in its plenary inspiration, and therefore in its essential, organic unity. There is only one Bible, however many authors and compilers we may recognize. What one part of the Bible says does not contradict what another part says; indeed, it is one of the key rules of interpretation that we use each part to shed light on each other part.

But that means that our interpretation has to recognize the distinction Geerhardus Vos makes between biblical and systematic theology. It is a distinction of which I remind people and preachers continually: "Biblical theology draws a line of development. Systematic theology draws a circle."[7] Biblical interpreters are interested in both. That is, they locate each sentence in its unit within its book according to its place on the line of redemptive revelation history. They recognize that some insights of revelation come earlier than others, and that from its earliest stages the revelation progresses along the timeline of history in a cumulative way, widening the arc of knowledge and narrowing the focus of interest at the same time. Eventually there comes One who fulfills every promise, type, and prediction so that the Scriptures testify of Him (see Luke 24:27, 44).

But serious interpreters of Scripture also note that each word is located within the circle of systematic theology, so that earlier revelations in history of the nature of God, for example, are to be set side by side with the

---

7. Geerhardus Vos, *Biblical Theology* (Edinburgh: Banner of Truth, 2000), 16.

later disclosures of God to provide a scientific and systematic statement of who God is and what He is like. Exclusively redemptive-historical preaching fails to the extent that it overlooks the wider theological firmament in which every individual part of the biblical revelation shines, shedding its light on the meaning of the whole.

The Bible Is Covenant Revelation

The second controlling principle is that of covenant. It is irrefutable that the overarching theme—the big story, or metanarrative—of Scripture is that of "covenant." Otherwise, why do we use the word "testament" to describe the two parts of the Bible? The call of Abraham is not just a matter of historic interest: in Genesis 12:3 God pronounces a covenant blessing on Abraham and his descendants, and Paul tells us in Galatians that Jesus died in order to secure that blessing for the Gentiles (Gal. 3:14). For us to receive the Holy Spirit by faith is, according to the Bible, for us to come into the enjoyment of the covenant blessings that God pronounced when He preached the gospel beforehand to Abraham (Gal. 3:8).

Whether we are self-consciously preaching as covenant theologians or not, what we are preaching is the heart of God's covenant of grace. To call Christ the Mediator is not simply to speak of Him as a "go-between" serving God and man; it is to speak in explicitly covenantal categories (Heb. 9:15; 12:24). It was by the blood of the everlasting covenant that God raised Him from the dead (Heb. 13:20), and it is the blood of the covenant that is symbolized in our Communion service. "Covenant" is not a theme of biblical theology that we may dismiss; to preach the gospel is to inform about the covenant, to invite into the covenant, and to set forth the blessings of the covenant.[8] In a penetrating comment in this connection, Christopher J. H. Wright suggests that the Great Commission of Matthew 28:18–20, of which preaching is a fundamental element, "could be seen as a Christological mutation of the original Abrahamic commission—'Go…and be a blessing…and all nations on earth will be blessed through you.'"[9]

---

8. Cf. Hugh Martin, *The Atonement: In Its Relations to the Covenant, the Priesthood, the Intercession of Our Lord* (Edinburgh: Knox Press, 1976), 20–21: "The gospel call comes forth from the covenant, and summons sinners into it. It is a voice from within the covenant, addressed to those that are without, with the view of bringing them within."

9. Christopher J. H. Wright, *The Mission of God: Unlocking the Bible's Grand Narrative* (Downers Grove, Ill.: IVP Academic, 2006), 213.

Preaching is a covenantal activity. That is to say, it sets before men and women the claims of God's truth and presses home on them the obligation to obey. To call men sinners is to highlight that they are covenant breakers; to call Jesus a Savior is to call Him a covenant maker; to assure Christians of their security in Christ is to call God a covenant keeper. The first announcement of the gospel in Genesis 3:15, to which I have already referred, is actually structured around the three great covenants. There is a need for the serpent to be crushed because the covenant of works has been broken; there is a promise that the seed of the woman will crush him because the covenant of redemption has provided it so; and there is the hope of deliverance through the bruising of the seed of the woman because the covenant of grace has taken up the strain and will deal with man's loss through the death of the Savior.

It is not enough to say that there is a general unity in Scripture: the unity is federal and covenantal. That means it is personal; if we have failed to make the words of God a speaking of His heart to ours, we have failed in our task. The words that are the building blocks of our sermons are covenant words, and it will give our sermons robustness and solidity if we recognize this.

The Bible Is Christ Revelation
The Scriptures testify about Jesus (John 5:39). He could preach Himself from them (Luke 24:44). It was His Spirit who spoke in and through the Old Testament prophets (1 Peter 1:10–11). It is in the word written and inscripturated that the Word eternal and incarnate gives Himself over to us.

Our preaching, therefore, takes as its default position that it is Christ we are to preach (1 Cor. 1:23). It is our task, as we deal with the meaning of the words before us, to find the natural lines of revelation that take us from text to Savior, from the words to the Word. We need not force the text out of its natural genre or meaning in order to do so. We need not resort to allegorizing the text or forcing a meaning into it. We simply recognize that the flow of the biblical narrative works in two directions, the Old Testament anticipating the coming of Christ and the New explaining it.

This used to be called a "Christocentric" reading of Scripture: a recognition that Christ is at the heart of the biblical revelation. Then it became known as a "Christotelic" reading: a seeing of Christ as the end to which the revelation was pointing. But neither designation is satisfactory even though both positions are true. Christ *is* at the Bible's heart, and He *is* at the Bible's end. But not without reason is the Word designated "the Alpha and the Omega" (Rev. 1:8; 21:6; 22:13): Christ is not just the Bible's meaning, but the Bible's alphabet. He is the Word that gives meaning to all its words, the *Logos* which supplies its logic, and the Truth that verifies its truth. Better to speak of Christ being the fullness of Scripture than simply its center or its end. Our sermon construction, therefore, takes its starting point not only from our understanding of its language but also from our being constrained both by the covenantal form of its revelation and the christological nature of its content.

In our handling of the Bible's words, we are recognizing the thoughts in which these words are dressed. Words, after all, are only the dress of thoughts. In the act of revelation that gave us the Bible, God clothed His ideas in Hebrew words and then in Greek words. These need to be translated and interpreted if we are to get to the key ideas being revealed: insights from the God of heaven who "reveals deep and secret things" (Dan. 2:22). There is a mystery that was "kept secret since the world began but [has] now [been] made manifest, and by the prophetic Scriptures [has been] made known to all nations…for obedience to the faith" (Rom. 16:25–26). Paul establishes the link between the revelation of the mystery and the preaching of the gospel in Ephesians 3:1–10 and reminds us that our sermons ought to be insights into the mind of God Himself, enabling us to think God's thoughts after Him.

Of course there is a fundamental assumption in all this that the Bible's ideas correspond to reality; they are not fantasy or make-believe; they are not fictional or mythical. When the Bible says that God created the heavens and the earth, or states that the Word who was in the beginning became flesh, or says that Jesus is risen from the dead, we believe that these are meanings and ideas that have a root in history and are incapable of falsification. Some ideas must be taken by faith and are beyond our ability to verify empirically, but they are no less true for that reason. The ideas in our sermons have their conception in the Bible's primary revelation of them.

Sermon preparation, therefore, includes not only knowing the meanings of words but also the concepts and meanings conveyed by the words, comprehending the ideas, big and small, which are scaffolded by them. The point of our sermon ought to be the point of our text, and it ought to convey, as clearly and as simply as possible, the idea of the text in all its biblical proportion and dimensions.

And the big idea in the text of Scripture at every point is that there is a person who reveals God to us and in whom we are complete: the Lord Jesus Christ. The stated aim of John's writing his gospel is that we will believe that

Jesus is Messiah, the Son of God, and through believing we will have life in Him (John 20:31). That is the aim of all Scripture, since the Bible testifies of Jesus (John 5:39). There is no part of the Bible which is not designed to lead us to the person and work of Jesus Christ.

Articulating the Word

In Luke 24:32, the risen Christ "opens" the word to the two with whom He walks on the Emmaus road. In the same chapter He opens the understanding of the disciples to appreciate the way in which the Old Testament spoke of Him (Luke 24:45). Charles H. Spurgeon says of this phenomenon that in the first of these Jesus has many helpers, but in the second He stands alone.[10] Only He can open the minds of men and women to appreciate the beauties of the biblical text, but He does this by the medium of preaching and through the act of having the Scriptures opened up and their meaning exposed. So, as fellow laborers of Christ, how are we to articulate the riches of the Word of God?

First, we open up the Scriptures *by identifying the main theme of the passage* on which we are preaching. Our sermons must have portability; we do not want to make them so heavy and overloaded that they fall between pews and stay there. Nor do we want to make them so light and airy that they float to the ceiling like a helium balloon. We want to make them portable so that they may be carried out by our hearers and remembered by them.

The key to making them portable is to focus them around the theme that is dominant in the passage of Scripture before us. This is one reason why preaching on an isolated text may be preferable to preaching on an extended passage. The idea of the verse ought to be the theme of the sermon. And it ought to be possible to state the theme of the sermon in one sentence.

I do not always give titles to my sermons beyond what is in the text on which I am preaching, but if I am posting the sermon online it is often necessary to do so. That is what tests the sermon's portability. It can sometimes be more difficult to find a title that encapsulates the main thought of the sermon than to fill out the sermon with thoughts and ideas. Yet the sermon should arise organically out of the text itself, and its main theme ought to be the main theme of the text.

As an element of speaking, articulation has to do with clarity and distinctness. The theme of our Bible text or passage ought to be clear and distinct

---

10. Charles H. Spurgeon, *Morning and Evening* (London: Marshall, Morgan, and Scott, 1974), reading for January 19.

too. In sermon preparation we are not trying to impose an alien theme onto a biblical text; rather, we are simply identifying and extracting the theme that is there. And it is in the detail of that theme that Christ will come to us, clothed in His own words and speaking with His own accent.

Second, we open the Scriptures *by identifying the contours of the framework* in which that theme is displayed. The love of God is the major theme of John 3:16, and it is also the major theme of Jude 21. But the framework of both verses is different. In John 3:16, the love of God is set before us as the basis of the gospel, as Jesus highlights that God loved us, what God loved, how He loved, and to what end He loved. In Jude, the context is different, as Jude exhorts God's people to keep themselves in the love of God, building in their faith, praying in the Spirit, and waiting for the mercy of Christ. Jude's language is explicitly Trinitarian, as he brings the doctrine of the triune God to bear on the matter of daily Christian living.

In other words, we recognize that the theme of our text is displayed within different frameworks and for different ends. And we need to see the distinct ways in which the theme is expressed. The main framework thoughts or doctrines will provide a setting for the theme and will therefore provide a shape for our sermon. There is no use in preaching a four-point sermon from a three-point text!

The Bible has quite a variety of "frames" for displaying its themes. The theme of the love and mercy of God can be expressed in narrative (such as in the Joseph narrative of Genesis), or in poetry (as in the Psalms or the Song of Solomon), or in didactic passages (like Deuteronomy 7:6–26), or in prophetic passages (like Hosea 11), or in gospel narratives (like John 17), or in epistolary form (such as in Romans 8:39 or Galatians 2:20). The context of these references to God's love is different in each case, so preaching on this common theme from these distinctive passages will shape the sermon in different ways.

That, at last, is the glory of preaching the Word of God; each passage in its own place and in its own way will bring us closer to the heart of God and closer to the mind of Christ. It is by hearing that faith comes (Rom. 10:17). The vision that faith gives is fed by the word that God gives.

Third, the Scriptures are opened *as we identify the trajectories of revelation* along which the theme is developed in Scripture. This links to an earlier comment—that the Bible is organic. Its themes, doctrines, and insights run parallel to each other. No part monopolizes any of its themes. Jesus preached from Moses onward all the things that concerned Himself; He was in every part.

To read the sermons of the great Puritans is to see this in practice. The Puritans recognized that the whole Scripture is designed to shed light on any particular part of Scripture, and therefore the theme of any one verse has a direct relation to the disclosure of the same theme elsewhere. Puritan preachers often seem to have ransacked the Bible for concepts and formulations related to the text they were expounding.

One result of this is that often their illustrations are taken from Scripture itself, and not necessarily from the world outside. That is not to say that there are no homely illustrations in Puritan sermons—quite the opposite. But it is to emphasize that the material within Scripture provides illustration and illumination enough to enable preachers to clarify the teaching of one part with the teaching of another. No amount of combing the culture for sermon illustrations can substitute for illustrating Scripture with Scripture itself.

Fourth, we open the Scriptures *by unpacking the contents of the theme.* Matthew describes the scribe "instructed concerning the kingdom of heaven" like "a householder who brings out of his treasure things new and old" (Matt. 13:52). Some scholars believe that Matthew is describing his own calling in that verse; whether that is the case or not he is certainly describing the calling of those who preach the Word. We will discover in our study of the text that there are old things there that are to be continually repeated; we will discover new things there that our people may never have heard before. At all times we will discover that the treasure, whether new or old, is always treasure and of peerless value.

Above all, we will find that in the treasure of Scripture is always the "pearl of great price" (Matt. 13:46), Jesus Himself. By opening up the riches of God's Word we are simply holding up that jewel and turning it around so that its contours, facets, and shapes will be clearly seen. That is what Jesus did on the Emmaus road, and it is what we must do too. Beginning with the words, we must end at the Word, for all the words of Scripture derive their significance from Him.

Conclusion

With different personalities and giftedness, preachers will develop different ways of approaching the task of sermon preparation. They will make their own different uses of the original languages, of translation, of concordance, and of vocabulary. They will have different approaches to the ways in which the texts of Scripture are to be mined for their gold and will have differing aptitudes when it comes to the use of words and the force of nuance and of meaning.

But we are surely all agreed that it is invidious to offer to the Lord that which costs us nothing (see 2 Sam. 24:24). The proclamation of His Word is worthy of our endeavors to wrestle with the text in which He has spoken to His people. We are recipients of His message, set apart to be heralds of His truth. The preaching of God's Word deserves our careful attention. May God raise up many other faithful heralds of the gospel like our brother Dr. Steven J. Lawson, who will pay attention to the opening up of God's Word for the benefit and blessing of Christ's church.

CHAPTER 12

Building the Sermon

Geoffrey Thomas

The pulpit from which I have preached for fifty years is my second home. It has two chairs (one is for visiting ministers). It is wide and I move about. It also contains a couple of small tables—one for Bibles and the other for the hymnbook—notices, a bottle of water, and a glass. It is carpeted, and there is an essential light above the lectern to shine on my notes and on the Scriptures. It is high enough for me to see the gallery, so that I don't have to crane my neck looking up and away to those who unfortunately sit up there (as there is always room for them within the body of the church downstairs). The pulpit is also high enough so that the congregation can see me across the heads of the people in front of them. Like many pastor-preachers I am most at ease in this second home where I proclaim the message that grace has enabled me to build during the previous week. It is the scene of my greatest blessings and griefs.

The congregation is called "God's building" (1 Cor. 3:9). Paul tells the Ephesian church that in Christ "the whole building, being fitted together, grows into a holy temple in the Lord, in whom you also are being built together for a dwelling place of God in the Spirit" (Eph. 2:21–22). My task is to build up this people—in fact, to make every effort to excel in gifts that build up the church (1 Cor. 14:12). That is my personal teleology, and to further it God provides all His called preachers with their necessary gifts. Christians are tempted to be like Sarai, who once said to Abram, "The LORD has restrained me from bearing children. Please, go in to my maid; perhaps I shall obtain children by her" (Gen. 16:2). There is no shortage of the devices that men will use in their attempts to build numerically the household of God. Like Sarai's strategy, these devices flow from a lack of faith, and they result in declension. The Son of God will build His church in His way; there is no other. He is present always in God's building, and to grieve Him by ignoring His ways will result in building without Him. That is like building without an architect, foreman, or skilled builders. One is building a ruin. A flood will quickly destroy it.

The principal means by which the house of God grows is through the Bible. The climactic aspect of our meetings together, after we have sung and prayed to God, is the Lord responding by addressing us through His called and gifted servants preaching the Bible to His people. So the beautiful household of faith grows in love, joy, and peace as the gospel of Jesus Christ comes to them, not in word only but also in power by the Holy Spirit and with much assurance. Let's think of this building and the preaching of the Word of God as the means of its erection and growth.

The Path That Leads to the House of God: The Preacher

The Christian life is called "the Way" a half dozen times in the book of Acts: a way of life, a way through the wilderness of the world, the pilgrim's way from the City of Destruction to the Celestial City, the narrow way that leads to life which only a few are able to find. The preacher has to be on that way. That is the first essential when discussing a call of God with a man contemplating the ministry. Is he on the Way? Has he left the City of Destruction? Has he experienced the new birth?

The first ambassador for the living God an inquirer may see is the preacher. The first words he may hear from him are "Let us pray," and the first thing he may listen to is this preacher's conversation with the Creator of heaven and earth. "He is speaking to the Maker of heaven and earth," he thinks, and he will listen with interest, quick to spot any artificiality of tone, of overfamiliarity, or groveling, lugubrious affectation. He is manly and affectionate and meek before El Shaddai. The inquirer will watch him leading the service, and he will hear his preaching. The minister's personality and manner will either enhance what the stranger hears or detract from it. You are embodying the Way; you are making it attractive or not. Men came to hear John Calvin and could not but notice that he ended every one of his thousands of sermons thus, "And now let us bow down before the majesty of our gracious God." That was his relationship with the God he preached to them. He was not a stiff-necked man; he was a bowing man. His God was majestic but gracious. The preaching of the Word was the way by which the congregation was to enter the house of God.

So the path to effective sermon building is in direct proportion to the healthy vigor of the redeemed humanity of the man of God. So he has to be an example in the basics of the faith. He must be above reproach. There is a clear cause-and-effect relationship between what a servant of God is as a man and what he accomplishes as a minister of the Word. The path to God is by a man joined to Christ, not one who is building by communication gimmicks and can hold a crowd and keep them entertained. It is by a holy man of God that God builds up His people, and particularly by his sermons. So we build ourselves up before we build our sermons.

In the opening pages of *Lectures to My Students*, Charles H. Spurgeon says,

> We are, in a certain sense, our own tools, and therefore must keep ourselves in order. If I want to preach the gospel, I can only use my own voice; therefore I must train my vocal powers. I can only think with my own brains, and feel with my own heart, and therefore I must educate my intellectual and emotional faculties. I can only weep and agonize for souls in my own renewed nature, therefore must I watchfully maintain the tenderness which was in Christ Jesus. It will be vain for me to stock my library, or organize my societies, or project schemes, if I neglect the culture of myself; for books, and agencies, and systems, are only remotely the instruments of my holy calling; my own spirit, soul, body, are my nearest machinery for sacred service; my spiritual faculties and my inner life, are my battle axe and weapons of war.[1]

The minister is the path to the household of faith, and that path must be more than level and tidy, illuminated in the night and lacking in stumbling blocks. It must be a path of eminent attractiveness in righteousness and Christlikeness. Here is someone full of the Holy Spirit and joy, all his mind and powers being dedicated to building up a congregation through building messages from the Word of God—sermons that are alive, strengthening, saving, and sanctifying—so all his powers are absolutely consecrated to the service of God. This man does one thing—and that is to be made conformable to the image of Christ. He devotes himself to the high office to which he is called. His great goal is to save men, and he thus has a more than ordinary interest in the souls of men. He is to be a leader of the people of God and to be an example in spiritual attainments. He must think like this: "All Christians, including myself, are the path to God, the appointed means God uses to reach the dying world, but if I am a minister of the gospel and have

---

1. Charles H. Spurgeon, *Lectures to My Students* (Grand Rapids: Zondervan, 1954), 7–8.

extraordinary privileges to serve that end, then surely I must be an example to the flock and rise higher in repentance, and prayerfulness and trust in Jesus Christ."

If we preachers are men's first sight and sound of a man of God, then our personal holiness and spiritual growth must be our primary vocation. If we are to effectively build sermons we ourselves must be built up day by day in our most holy faith.

The Door That Enters the Household of God: The Text

The door into the household of God for many strangers is the word of God that a preacher is bringing to him in the context of a believing, worshiping fellowship of Christians. They are all listening, but the favored stranger in particular will hear this word at an appointed time. At the set time of God the word from heaven comes to him. You, the preacher, have had him in mind (and others as well) as you have been considering the text you have decided to open up on this occasion. There is a mystery here. The romance of it has gone for many because they are locked into systematic expository preaching morning and evening, and they have thrown away the key to entering into any other method of preaching. They have known what they are to preach on from breakfast time on the preceding Monday, but for others the gift of a text comes from the love of God.

What, then, about the choice of the text? In many ways this is so important and where I feel a considerable sense of failure. Every preacher is confronted by the challenge of choosing a text. Twice every Sunday, twice next Sunday, twice on the following Sunday with just the occasional visit to another pulpit. How many of us go through that? It is a privilege and a responsibility. The question of the choice of texts is a critical one and attention should be given to it at once and continuously. How is a man to choose texts? Texts are sometimes chosen out of our regular reading, sometimes they are taken up in order to deal with some special need, sometimes in order to define doctrinal teachings, and sometimes because of their revelation of great things.

This is what G. Campbell Morgan records:

> By "text" we meant the paragraph, the verse, or part of a verse, which is the basis of a sermon.... From my own experience I may say that in the regular reading of the Bible devotionally, there will constantly be discovered some one text, some one statement, some one verse, which grips. When such is the case let us never hurry on. It is good to stop

and put it down. Postpone further reading, until we have at least said to ourself, Why did that arrest me; what is there in that which pulled me up? Make a note of it: If we form the habit of constantly doing that in our devotional reading we shall find these things that thus seemed to leap out at us. "When found, make a note of"—Captain Cuttle's advice is very excellent. If possible we should make an outline of the scheme of thought suggested. Sometimes when we want a text, we shall run over these outlines, and perhaps not see a thing in ninety-nine per cent of them. In one per cent we shall, and that one per cent is worthwhile.

Sometimes a text will bring a ready-made sermon. That is not often the case, but it is so now and then. It is not merely a message but a whole scheme.[2]

This counsel clearly impacted Martyn Lloyd-Jones, co-pastor with Morgan for a few years, as we learn from similar exhortations in his book *Preaching and Preachers* to do the same thing. He even explains how he came to preach his famous series on spiritual depression.

I have explained to you how you can accumulate a large number of skeletons. I had been doing this for a number of years and so I had a pile of skeletons. What happened on that occasion, while I was dressing that morning was that I was shown that in my pile of skeletons there was a ready-made series on spiritual depression. It was not that the whole pile dealt with this, but that in the pile there were odd sermons that could be put in order to form a series. This was to me such a remarkable experience that I have never forgotten it, and never shall.[3]

So in some way you have a text. Then what? How do you build on the design and materials provided for you in this unique text of Scripture? Note the excellent advice of Stuart Olyott:

On your knees, literally! Now read your text. Take it sentence by sentence, word by word, using every part as fuel for prayer. Yes, concentrate on the text to the exclusion of everything else; avoid all (all!) interruptions; brood on the text in the Lord's presence. Worship him for every truth and lesson that you see. If there is any part of the text and lesson that you do not understand, pray, brood and meditate until you do. If light still does not come, consult your commentaries and other

---

2. G. Campbell Morgan, *Preaching* (New York: Fleming H. Revell, [1937]), 39, 43.
3. Martyn Lloyd-Jones, *Preaching and Preachers* (Grand Rapids: Zondervan, 1971), 195.

aids—but only to find out what this phrase or sentence means, and nothing more.

As you wait upon God, thoughts will begin to come, perhaps slowly at first. But one thought will suggest another, and this in turn will lead to another. Stay on your knees until the passage inflames your soul—until the fire burns, making you impatient to preach the truths which you have now made your own, and especially the "big idea," that is, the dominant thought which sums up what the text is about. You have not asked for a message. But the Word of God is now enthusing you and the direction of your message is clear.

Go to your desk and ask your text questions. Write down the answers. Don't try at this stage to arrange anything into any logical sequence—this can be done later. Take time to do this work thoroughly—paper is not in short supply and you can use lots of it, if necessary. First of all, ask these basic questions:

What is the immediate, wider and historical context?

What did this text mean to the author and to the original hearers?

And what does it have to say today?

What does it teach about God, the Father, the Son, the Holy Spirit?

What does it teach about men, their attitude to God and to each other?

Is there a good example to follow, or a bad one to avoid?

Is there a command to obey?

Is there a warning to heed?

Is there a promise to believe and proclaim?

Is there an answer to a biblical or personal question?

Is there some teaching to take particularly to heart?

Is there a teaching confirmed by other passages of the Bible?[4]

---

4. Stuart Olyott, *Preaching: Pure and Simple* (Bridgend, Wales: Bryntirion Press, 2005), 169–79.

The Hallway: The Introduction to the Sermon

You step across the doorway into the hall, and you immediately get a taste of the house. There are family photographs on the walls, doors leading into other rooms, the smell of cooking, the noise of a radio, and children playing. You are now inside and soon to be introduced to more. Every sermon must also have a point of entry. How do you introduce the sermon?

One of my favorite preachers who has spoken often and written helpfully about preaching fails spectacularly (in my judgment) in his introductions. He can often start by rehearsing at length all he said in the previous message. How wearying that is! Please keep the introduction short. Once the drill has hit the artesian well, then you stop drilling. A woman said of a Welsh preacher that he was so long in spreading the table she had lost her appetite for the meal. Your hallway may be tastefully decorated with a fine mirror and coatrack and a picture of the family ten years old, but keeping guests standing there too long is not kind. The guest needs to enter the living room and meet the family. An introduction needs to be long enough to capture attention, raise needs, and fix listeners' attention on the theme, and then to escort them into the movement of the sermon.

No sermon should begin with an apology, for example, that you have not had the time to deal with this theme as it merits because of emergencies that occurred during the week. You are merely showing listeners how well you can speak with limited preparatory time at your disposal. If you have been helped by the sermon of another preacher, don't tell your listeners that in the opening sentence. Quote the man a few times or tell them what help you have had as you get into the preaching. And no introduction should promise more than it delivers. Do not tell the congregation that this theme is going to be the most important sermon they have ever heard. Don't tell them that this is wonderful—you hope they are going to marvel as you open up your message to them—or you have built them up to be disappointed. Sensational introductions to mediocre sermons are like broken promises. If you fail to meet the need you have raised, then the congregation will feel cheated.

Haddon W. Robinson, in his customary helpful way, says,

> Early in the sermon listeners should realize that the pastor is talking to them about themselves. The preacher raises a question, probes a problem, identifies a need, opens up a vital issue to which the passage speaks. Application starts in the introduction, not in the conclusion. Should a preacher of even limited ability bring to the surface people's questions, problems, hurts, and desires to deal with them from the Bible, he will

be acclaimed a genius. More important than that, he will through his preaching bring the grace of God to bear on the agonizing worries and tensions of daily life.[5]

A good introduction should perform four basic tasks, claims Stephen McQuoid:

1. It should gain the attention of the listener. As the Russian proverb says, "It is the same with men as with donkeys: whoever would hold them fast must get a very good grip of their ears." There is no need for the introduction to be dramatic, but you must aim to capture attention in the first thirty seconds.

2. It should secure interest, and then keep the audience listening. One admirable preacher from Liverpool frequently begins his sermons by speaking of a person whom he will give a name who is experiencing a testing time or knowing a great blessing or asking a very searching question. People sit up and listen at the prospect of a story. Here is one of Haddon Robinson's: "Mary Watson was a housewife in her late thirties. She thought of herself as young and still attractive even though she had been married for fifteen years and was the mother of three children. In the space of a month she developed into an ugly old woman."

   "What happened to her then?" we all ask, but Robinson does not tell us. The introduction must so captivate listeners that they want to hear more of what the speaker has to say.

3. It should provide a natural path into the subject matter. By the end of the introduction, the audience must understand exactly where the preacher is taking them. So after the preacher has completed the sermon, let him look again at his introduction and rewrite it because then he will have a better understanding of where he has taken his listeners.

4. It should warm the heart and prepare it to obey. The preacher is appealing to his congregation to listen to one part of the Word of God, convinced that this is the most relevant message they can possibly be hearing. Preaching is about movement; in other words, it is moving a congregation by the Word preached to walk more closely with God in the coming week. The preacher wants to motivate them

---

5. Haddon W. Robinson, *Expository Preaching: Its Principles and Practice* (Leicester: Inter-Varsity, 1986), 164.

by the Word, and that is more than declaring theological and biblical facts. Your aim in the next thirty minutes is to kindle a flame of sacred love in their hearts.[6]

There is no formula for the introduction. The preacher may start with a familiar thought in an unfamiliar setting. He may make a comment on some traumatic event that the country has been talking about during the past week. He may give a statistic, ask a rhetorical question, or make a provocative comment about his text. He may tell the people that these words are the most misunderstood in the Bible. The possibilities for introductions are as wide as your own personality and creativity. But the old proverb is true, "Well begun, half done."

The Living Room: The Place Where People Are Dealt with Personally

There are four preachers I have known whose gifts are such that immediately when they begin to speak the congregation relaxes. The people settle down and listen intently to what is being said. It is indubitably an endowment of God; it is also an elevated natural gift. It comes from the confidence of those four men in themselves, in their sense of calling, and in their ability to speak the word unafraid of men. It comes from knowing exactly what they are going to say, having it in their hearts, where it is bursting to come out. It comes from their skill in managing and handling men.

Addressing listeners in that relaxing manner is like inviting guests into your home, escorting them through the hall into the living room, sitting them in a comfy chair and engaging in conversation with them, putting them at their ease. The preacher begins to speak and prepares a congregation to deal with God and with themselves as God is seeing and helping them. Dr. Lloyd-Jones was one such preacher. I remember the last occasion he spoke in Wales. Every pew in the old chapel with its seven hundred places was taken, and he began. His text was Psalm 2. The time flew by, and soon he was exhorting us to do what the psalmist tells us: "Kiss the Son, lest He be angry, and you perish in the way" (v. 12). It was all over too soon, an hour disappearing like a watch in the night, and then we sang with all our hearts a great Welsh hymn tune. I quaveringly pronounced the benediction, and everyone sat down. No one was in a hurry to leave. We sat around for an hour

---

6. Stephen McQuoid, *The Beginner's Guide to Expository Preaching* (Fearn, Ross-shire, Scotland: Christian Focus, 2002), 119–20.

and stood in the quiet street on a warm May evening. The children gravitated toward one another, feeling that they were in on an event of significance. The adults thought rightly that we would never hear the beloved doctor preach again in the flesh, and so much we owed him. What a new work God did for Wales when He homed in on a medical student in London, England, in the 1920s. What new work will He do in our day when the nations are imagining other vain things?

The living room is the place you get to know the master of the house. And in the sermon the congregation gets to know God, then themselves, then why they need Him and can have Him by means of faith and repentance. The message has in the background exegetical biblical accuracy and confessional doctrinal substance. That is as essential as the foundations, beams, and wiring and heating vents that make the living room inviting and comfortable. Those properties are indispensable, but invisible. You do not speak about such details when you are together.

A clear structure to the encounter is also essential, though again attention is not drawn to that fact. We do not normally have on our laps a piece of paper with four headings that we take our guest through. A consciousness of that plan certainly will not relax them and open them to our gentle questions and shared opinions; nevertheless, we do have in our minds what direction we need to take in dealing with the visitor we have welcomed into our home. The preacher too is concerned about the structure of the sermon he is building. He has been moved by a passage from Holy Writ and wants to move others by its truths to love, wonder, and adore, and so his message must have unity, order, and proportion. No building can stand without such features, and neither can the sermon.

Stuart Olyott explains these terms:

> Preachers who love their people are fussy about the structure of their sermons. They know that the most ordinary person will never lose their way, as long as the sermon has unity, order and proportion. *Unity* means that the message all holds together; it is not made up of several disconnected sermonettes. *Order* means that the sermon is made of distinct ideas which follow each other in a logical chain that leads up to a climax. *Proportion* means that each idea is given its proper place; unimportant things are not magnified, and important things are not played down. The worst preacher on earth will improve immediately if he remembers these three words.

I have often been told that order is "heaven's first law." Certainly God is a God of order. Anyone who has ever reflected on the Holy Trinity knows that there is an order and symmetry within the being of God which is breathtaking in its beauty. Disorder is another word for ungodliness.[7]

So there is the introduction, and this flows into what has been called traditionally the discussion. It is the truth that must be explained and applied to these people now. It is composed of the material that you have set yourself to gather in this sermon on this particular passage of Scripture. Nothing anywhere else says it just like this passage. What is its uniqueness? Obviously you must have a major plan for the whole sermon and a number of mini-plans for your various subpoints. There is prearranged order. Oratory, remember, is all about movement—that is, you are leading your listeners in a certain direction with increased acceleration and understanding for the obedience of faith.

The plan of the sermon should be as simple as possible so that hearers can perceive where they are going. There are white lines on the road and reflectors at the center that help make everything simpler. There are large black and white arrows on bends preparing you before you start to turn the steering wheel. Your plan should be simple, but not simplistic. It must be natural, but not clever or quirky. It must not be monotonous, but neither do you want it to be coruscating. God alone gives the thunder and lightning. Listeners are hardly to take notice of the structure, but should subconsciously be aware that it is there.

Divisions are helpful. I like the congregation to know that we are progressing to another point. Olyott says that headings are like snow poles on a winter road, showing the plan of the road ahead and the edges. Our hearers can see the argument develop and to what point they have reached and where they are going next. The human mind is in God's image, the God of order and not chaos, and sermons without such development are likely to dehumanize people. Think of the logical development of Jesus's preaching of the Sermon on the Mount.

So divisions are to be distinct and progressive, each one leading to the next. They must be orderly and moving like an army going into battle. They must advance in strength as you progress, the argument gaining some

---

7. Olyott, *Preaching: Pure and Simple*, 75.

momentum as the current of thought is channeled, your hearers getting more keyed up about the coming climax. There should not be many divisions. There should be three. Occasionally there might be two or four, and very infrequently there might be nine! But generally there are three.

John M. Frame has said fascinating things about the number three. He writes, "The number three seems omnipresent in Scripture, nature, philosophy, and religion. I have catalogued hundreds of triads, including many that might be thought to reflect the Trinity in one way or another."[8] Vern S. Poythress carries the analogy further, finding a Trinitarian analogy in the triad of physical science—particle, wave, and field—applied to linguistics. Frame has an intricate appendix in his systematic theology simply listing hundreds of triads. So it is natural in building a sermon to make use of what God has put into His creation. But let the divisions of our sermons by prayer and thoughtfulness be made as attractive as they can, serving our cause of people knowing the Word of the Lord and the Lord of the Word.

The Dining Room: Where Together Affectionately We Eat

A meal is something animals know nothing about. Animals know about eating, for in their waking hours that is what they do almost constantly, but a meal is bringing together various people and different foods in balance and proportion in the context of affection and welcome with edifying, happy conversation and ministry to one another. It is not enough to serve a good diet of systematic, exegetical truths, perceived and enlightened by the insights of the history of redemption. There must be thoughtfulness in the building of the sermon for all who are present. For example, there are children present, and just as in a family mealtime the father does not need to apologize to those sitting around the table while he feeds spoonfuls of baby food into the hungry mouth of his one-year-old daughter, so we do not need to apologize when we choose to stretch the most mature saint with some keen biblical insights and application or when we say, "Children!" and then apply the truths of this word to them. Aren't the architect and builder aware that children also are going to be living in this building? If you were designing a lecture hall or a student union complex your approach would be altogether different. The sermon is built for all who attend.

---

8. John M. Frame, *Systematic Theology* (Phillipsburg, N.J.: P&R, 2013), 507.

A meal and a sermon last about the same time—forty minutes—and the buzz of the occasion speeds the time. The contribution of all who are present—watching, listening, and feeding on the meal you're serving—is crucial. "She is here…. He has come back" you think as you stand in the pulpit and see your congregation. How that helps in building the sermon.

And then you really don't know what you have built. Of course there are those rare sermons you will actually preach for a second time because of the combination of all that is best in them—the design, the windows, the beauty of Christ and His salvation—but that one message is a precious gift from God, maybe one in a year if God so blesses you. As for the rest, you cannot judge. You may even think it was a poor building, that sermon, an old hut worthy of demolition and better forgotten. Maybe another man thought the same. He had been called in suddenly on January 6, 1850, to occupy the pulpit at Artillery Street Primitive Methodist Church in Colchester after a snowstorm had prevented the expected man from turning up. There were a dozen or so in the congregation, including a teenage boy named Charles Haddon Spurgeon, who was there for the first time. The visiting preacher preached on the text, "Look unto me and be ye saved all the ends of the earth" and urged the congregation to do that very thing, repeating himself for about ten minutes. Then he ran out of steam and, turning his attention on the young Spurgeon, told him publicly that he looked miserable and always would be miserable until he looked to Jesus. Then it was all over, and they all went home, walking carefully through the icy streets. The preacher went home to his wife, we suppose, and when she asked him how it had gone, he might have told her there'd been a dozen people there, and he had told them all to look to Jesus. He never owned up to being the preacher of that forgettable sermon, though three others did. That very thin-looking man, a shoemaker or a tailor, carried on his trade for the rest of his life, unaware of what God had done that day in the heart of Charles Haddon Spurgeon. We simply don't know what good has been done with our frequent poor sermons, but we said a word of Jesus, and the day will reveal it. I am looking forward to meeting Spurgeon in glory—but also the man who built that sermon on January 6, 1850.

CHAPTER 13

Delivering the Sermon

Conrad Mbewe

I recall that Sunday as if it were yesterday, yet it was well over thirty years ago. I went to church as I always did, took my place in the front pew as I had done on many a Lord's Day, and got out my pen and notebook because it was now time to listen to the sermon. I cannot remember now what the sermon was about or what the text was. What I recall vividly was that in the midst of that sermon I lost consciousness of time and felt as if God had come down and was dealing with me personally. The power of the sermon was overwhelming and left me pleading with the living God for grace to live a life that truly glorifies Him. I left church that day praying, "O Lord, if You ever call me to preach, let me preach like that!"

Since then, I have listened to many sermons that have had a similar impact on me. I have also heard a few such testimonies with respect to my own preaching. As a homiletician, I have spent some time asking the question, What is it about the delivery of the sermon that makes it so powerful and puts it in a class of its own when compared to all other forms of live audio communication? This is the question that I seek to answer in this chapter.

Some Important Presuppositions

To begin with, we need to assume that a good sermon has been prepared. Each point is clearly stated. The sermon is simple in language and illustrates its main points appropriately where necessary. It has an arresting introduction, progresses in a consistent direction in its main body, and has a relevant conclusion. We are also assuming that the sermon being carried into the pulpit is faithful to the text of Scripture that it is based on, is christocentric, and has pertinent applications in each of its main points. So if anything goes wrong in the delivery of the sermon, at least we are assured that the fault did not lie in the sermon preparation. A good job has been done there.

Any preacher who has labored in the pulpit long enough will tell you that when you leave your study with a good sermon on paper, the arduous work of preaching is only half done. As important as sermon preparation might be, it is only half of the work. Many sermons that read well on paper often fall flat in the pulpit during their delivery. Also, the same sermon may be preached with great power in one place and sound like a university lecture in another. Part of the answer lies in the sovereign work of the Holy Spirit, as Daniel Webster Whittle wrote in 1883,

> I know not how the Spirit moves,
>> Convincing men of sin,
>> Revealing Jesus through the word,
>> Creating faith in him.[1]

So we must also assume that as a preacher, you go into the pulpit in utter dependence upon the Holy Spirit, that He may use you for His own glory. With all that "under the belt," we must still state that yet another part of the answer to effective preaching lies in how we deliver our sermons as preachers. This is what I seek to address here.

Three Major Goals of Preaching

To begin, we need to be clear about what we want to achieve as we enter the pulpit to deliver the sermon. Let me suggest three major goals:

1. *To inform the mind about God's truth and will.* Preaching is primarily a vehicle of communication. God has revealed Himself in creation, but He has also deliberately revealed Himself through His Word. So when we preach, we want to tell the world this information so that they not only may know the kind of God who is there but also may respond to this information about God appropriately.

2. *To inflame the heart with love for the truth.* This is the first appropriate response to the preaching of the Word of God. Men and women must find their hearts strangely warmed toward the truth of God and the God of that

---

1. D. W. Whittle, "I Know Not Why God's Wondrous Grace," 1883, public domain.

truth. To do the will of God without love for God and His ways is hypocrisy, and God detests it. So as we preach, we want those who hear us to obey the greatest commandment—to love the Lord.

3. *To inspire the will to do what God wants.* This is the ultimate goal of preaching. We do not simply want people to feel right; we want them to live right. True preaching should result in changed lives. Sin must be repented of. Relationships must be restored. Divine and human authorities must be obeyed. God must be worshiped in all things. This is what God wants to achieve through our preaching.

The first major goal is foundational to everything else. Informing the mind is largely the fruit of good sermon preparation because that is where you are piecing together the information that you will pass on to your hearers. It is in sermon preparation that you achieve a clear exposition and application of Scripture. The last two major goals are largely the fruit of good sermon delivery. Through your personality as a preacher, not only will God be informing the mind but He will also be inflaming the heart and inspiring the will of your listeners to obey Him. In that sense, sermon delivery must involve your whole person as a preacher, including all your faculties. Notice the place of the personality of the preacher in Haddon W. Robinson's definition of expository preaching: "Expository preaching is the communication of a biblical concept, derived from and transmitted through a historical, grammatical, and literary study of a passage in its context, which the Holy Spirit first applies to the personality of the preacher, then through him to his hearers."[2]

There are at least four areas of human personality that are involved in the delivery of the sermon: emotions, voice, gestures, and eyes. Your thoughts are conveyed through these four vehicles. Let us look at each one of them for our own instruction.

Your Emotions

Take it as a maxim that a preacher can be forgiven almost any fault other than a dull, boring, and heavy delivery.[3] People expect that a servant of God who is coming to address them about matters of eternal life and eternal death will at least be conspicuously earnest about the message he is bringing to them.

---

2. Haddon W. Robinson, *Biblical Preaching: The Development and Delivery of Expository Messages* (Grand Rapids: Baker Academic, 2001), 21.

3. Martyn Lloyd-Jones, *Preaching and Preachers* (Grand Rapids: Zondervan, 1971), 87.

This strong, heartfelt intensity is due to a combination of reverence about the matter at hand and liveliness in delivery. The apostle Paul reminded Titus to exhort young men to be sober-minded, "in all things showing yourself to be a pattern of good works; in doctrine showing integrity, reverence, incorruptibility" (Titus 2:7). It is this reverence together with vigor and dynamism that produce the emotion of earnestness in preaching.

The emotion of earnestness must never be affected. Rather, it must come from the impact of the message upon your own soul. The subject that you are going to preach on must possess you. That is why it is vital for a preacher to have a few moments of prayerful silence and meditation before he preaches. He needs to shut himself up with the God who has given him His message so that he can once again sense the gravity of the task that is before him as he speaks to dying men as a dying man himself. In those moments of solitude, he is seeking to be gripped by the message that he is about to proclaim, knowing that only as the message has an impact upon his own soul will it also impact those who hear him. Or, to put it in concrete terms, in those quiet moments he is seeking to be welded to his sermon so that as he preaches it he and his sermon will be one.

Another way to look at this is the recognition that as a preacher you are an ambassador of the King of kings and Lord of lords. He sends you into His world in order for you to announce to the world the message from heaven to a people who need to hear it on earth. Understanding this to any measure will inevitably have a profound effect on you and the way in which you preach. The apostle Paul said, "Now then, we are ambassadors for Christ, as though God were pleading through us: we implore you on Christ's behalf, be reconciled to God" (2 Cor. 5:20). Notice the words he uses: "God…pleading through us," and "we implore you on Christ's behalf." Those are not words representing someone droning along half asleep and giving you a message with an I-don't-care attitude. No, there is an emotional attachment to what he has to say! And what is his message? It is one that demands a verdict: "Be reconciled to God!" Inevitably, therefore, you will preach with emotions when you recognize this awesome responsibility that as a preacher you are an ambassador of Christ, bringing His message of reconciliation to a rebellious world.

Your Voice

Your voice is the irreducible minimum that you use in your sermon delivery. Without a voice you cannot preach. There are other forms of communication, and through those forms you can pass on the word of God to others.

For instance, you can use sign language. You can write and publish what you want people to know. You can call that teaching if you want. But preaching demands that you lift your voice and proclaim the oracles of God. That is how the first sermon in the book of Acts is cited: "But Peter, standing up with the eleven, raised his voice and said to them, 'Men of Judea and all who dwell in Jerusalem, let this be known to you, and heed my words'" (Acts 2:14). This "raised" voice is essential to true preaching.

One of the many stories that has made its rounds about Charles Haddon Spurgeon, the great nineteenth-century preacher, is of a young man who came to tell him that he had sensed a call to the preaching ministry. The young man could hardly speak loud enough to be heard. He said, "Mr. Spurgeon, I think that God is calling me to become a preacher." Spurgeon, who himself had a voice that could be heard clearly in a room with ten thousand people without a public address system, leaned forward and in a voice that was as low as a whisper said to the young man, "I don't think so." Spurgeon's argument was that if God intended the young man to become a preacher, He would have given him the voice to do so. After all, He who creates us is also the One who later calls us to serve Him.

So never underestimate the gift that God has given you in your voice. You have a unique voice. It is like no one else's. It has its own pitch, its own penetrating power, its own flexibility, its own accent, and its own sweetness. When you were young, your mother would identify that it was you crying simply by the sound of your voice. In adulthood, your friends can tell that you are in the next room simply by your voice. It is that voice that will identify you as a preacher.

The role that your voice will play is, first, communicating the words of your sermon. People need to hear what God wants to tell them through you. Hence, it is vital that you learn to speak in such a way as to be heard properly. For some people, this is not a problem. Yet many people have picked up bad speech habits along the way as they have grown up. If you are in this latter category, the future of your preaching ministry hangs on your learning to overcome those bad speech habits. Sometimes the bad habits are cultural. They reflect how everyone speaks in that part of the world. Perhaps they just never pronounce the consonants at the end of words, and they somehow have learned to understand each other. However, as a preacher you will not preach only to people in your region. God may call you to minister elsewhere, or your sermons may be uploaded onto the Internet and listened to by people around the world. And so it is important that you unlearn those bad speech habits for the sake of greater usefulness.

In the age of public address systems, too many people talk to the microphone instead of speaking through it. This is a modern-day curse. Too many otherwise good sermons have been killed by this error. The public address system is an aid and not a replacement to proper effort in preaching. It is simply meant to amplify your voice beyond your normal level. It is not meant to be an excuse for you to now lower your voice out of sheer laziness. If the room you are speaking in is small, let the sound technician lower the amplification to almost zero instead of you reducing your voice to a mere whisper. Every preacher should learn to throw his voice by using his God-given diaphragm together with his lungs. He must be seen to be preaching, and not simply saying words.

Part of the reason a preacher must be allowed to make use of the full breadth of his voice is because, apart from communicating words, the voice also communicates emotional intensity. What you are saying in your sermon sometimes needs to be said with passion. You feel it strongly in your soul, and you want to communicate that feeling through your voice. As your sermon progresses and the emotions build up, so also will the intensity coming through your voice. In written communication you can use bold or italicized words or you can use an exclamation mark at the end of the sentence to communicate that intensity. You do not have that luxury in verbal or audio communication. Your voice does all that by communicating the intensity of what you have to say.

One error of young preachers is confusing intensity with loudness. If there was an error I was ever guilty of in my own preaching, this was it! I was hardly ever conscious of it because I have been gifted with a loud voice. However, older preachers would often bring it to my attention. I am not even sure that I have totally overcome it. I guess most of the older preachers have since passed on to glory. I am now in the category of "older preachers" myself. So on this I am speaking to myself as well as to you, my readers. Loudness causes pain in the hearers' ears, and so they try to shut you out in self-protection. They become so preoccupied with how to listen to you comfortably that in the process they miss the actual message you are seeking to communicate to them. Loudness also distorts words so that your hearers cannot understand what you are saying. As a general rule, speak at decibel levels that are comfortable to the ears even when your emotions are very high.

Another error to run away from like a plague is haranguing your hearers. What does that mean? This is a form of angry verbal communication that scolds and shouts at people. The person speaking is often ranting and berating his hearers. It is a form of emotional abuse, to say the least. People who sit under such "preaching" are psychologically tortured until they are too emotionally drained to think for themselves. Sadly, many people mistake this for preaching. It is not. That kind of ranting must stop. It gives preaching a bad name. Those who come to hear you should hear you gladly. That is what was said of the preaching of John the Baptist and of our Lord Jesus Christ. People heard them gladly (Mark 6:20; 12:37).

Another error that needs to be corrected is that of accent imitation. This is often an unconscious error on the part of a protégé. In listening a lot to the "master" you pick up some of his speech mannerisms and begin to sound like a poor imitation of the original. While this can be pardoned for a young preacher who is yet to cut his teeth in his vocation, it is inexcusable for an older preacher. As soon as possible in your preaching career you need to learn to be comfortable in your own skin. You must sound like yourself.

This is a common error in Africa. We listen so much to American preachers. Hence, many of our African preachers have taken on an American accent with a Southern drawl. More recently, Nigerian preachers have been taking the continent by storm. Hence, it is not uncommon to come across preachers in other African countries sounding like Nigerians. It is not until you read their names that you discover they are from another part of Africa. There is nothing spiritual about an American or Nigerian accent. What matters is that the people you are preaching to can hear you clearly. Remember, neither John the Baptist nor the Lord Jesus Christ had an American or Nigerian accent, yet people came to them in throngs and heard them gladly.

One last error is being monotonous. "Monotone" refers to a single tone (like the droning sound that a bee makes), but I am using this word in its widest and most general sense. The volume range that God has put in the human voice is incredible. Your voice can go from a soft whisper to a loud shout. The pace at which you speak is yet another form of elasticity that God has given you. You can leisurely stroll, briskly walk, and even jog or run with your voice. You can also prolong words as part of giving them emphasis. Your voice has astonishing variety in pitch and ictus. All these are God-given characteristics in the human voice that must not be suppressed.

I have heard people read exciting passages of Scripture with such monotone that I have been tempted to pull them off the podium so that I could do it myself. Imagine someone reading in a monotone the words of the disciples to whom Jesus had revealed Himself on the road to Emmaus as they returned to their friends and announced, "The Lord is risen indeed, and has appeared to Simon!" (Luke 24:34). It is almost criminal. There is no doubt that there was excitement and thrill in their voices. That excitement and intensity must be communicated to your hearers as you read the text. To put it succinctly, kill monotone before monotone kills your preaching!

Your Gestures

Another vehicle by which you communicate in sermon delivery is your gestures. The movements of your body and your facial expressions are an important part of your preaching. They often communicate your thoughts and emotions without your even realizing it. Whereas your voice communicates your thoughts and emotions through the ear gate, your gestures communicate your thoughts and emotions through the eye gate. When the two augment each other, your preaching is aided rather than obstructed. For instance, you can tell when a person is angry both by the intensity in his voice (if you are sitting in the next room) and his facial expression (when you are facing him). You will agree that being in the presence of a person who is fuming is a more fearful experience than simply hearing his angry words.

Preaching must involve your whole body, from the head all the way down to the toes. Granted, not every part of your body will be visible to your hearers, but your whole body must be so coordinated that it becomes one missile with deadly focus. There is no doubt that those who harness the full potential of the members of their bodies in the great act of sermon delivery are by far better preachers than those who have not done so. Spurgeon spoke of some pulpits as coffins where preachers are buried up to their necks. Pulpits that are so high that all the people can see is the preacher's head disfavor the act of preaching. Enough needs to be seen of the preacher's gestures to give the eye gate the opportunity to see the sermon; it is not enough that only the ear gate hears it.

The most common form of gestures in preaching is facial expressions. The general rule here is that facial expressions must represent the issue at hand at that point in the sermon. Are you speaking about joy at that point in your sermon? A smile rather than a frown on your face is surely the body language that best augments what you are speaking about. Are you warning your congregation about the wrath of God against sin? A serious look on your face should send a clear signal that this is no joking matter. Facial expressions can take away from what you are saying instead of augmenting it. Where you feel what you are speaking about with true spiritual integrity, you should not worry about your facial expression. That will certainly take care of itself. This is why it is important to prayerfully meditate on your sermon prior to entering the pulpit to preach it. You need to be in sympathy with the subject that you will be preaching about. Your facial expressions will inevitably follow.

The use of your arms and hands in preaching ranks second to facial expressions as an aid to preaching. Preachers who hold on to the pulpit throughout most of their sermon delivery deny themselves this in their preaching. It is only natural when a person is speaking that he will use his arms all the way from his shoulders to his hands. For instance, we often shrug our shoulders, hold out our arms, and even turn our palms upward when denying something. That augments what we are saying. Many preachers point their fingers in the direction of what they are talking about. Again, this augments what they are saying. What matters is that you should be natural. The use of your arms should not look as if you are acting because that will be a distraction.

What we need to realize about gestures is that we often communicate a message to our hearers through them even when we do not intend to. Gestures are normally unconscious expressions on our part. Hence, in pastoral counseling, we often can tell the state of people we are counseling simply by their body movements. We can tell if they are nervous or relaxed. We can tell if they are uncomfortable about the subject we have broached simply by how they shift their eyes or how they keep moving in their chair. Sometimes a distant look in their eyes tells us we are not connecting with them. In the same way, we communicate different thoughts, emotions, and attitudes to our hearers by our bodily gestures. Our body language betrays us.

One body language that is distracting in sermon delivery is that which says to your hearers that you are nervous. It causes your hearers to feel sorry for you, so they miss the message you are conveying to them. Nervousness causes your hands and arms to be in awkward places. You are ever fidgeting and fiddling with your sermon notes. Your eyes also tend to dart all over the place because you are trying to avoid looking anyone in the face. Whereas some level of nervousness will be normal if you are in an august assembly for the first time, it is important that you do something about it early enough in your sermon so that it is not a distraction. You have an important message to deliver from the King of kings and Lord of lords. You dare not be a distraction to your hearers. In fact, often when you remember the One you are representing, your nervousness is quickly killed. When you preach you are doing so in the name of the Lord Jesus Christ. He is the one who said, "All authority has been given to Me in heaven and on earth. Go therefore and make disciples of all the nations" (Matt. 28:18–19). Meditating upon that truth will go a long way to cure any preacher of prolonged nervousness.

What will not be cured by meditation are mannerisms. We all have them. Some of them can be unconscious aids to our preaching, but many of them are detrimental. I have a friend who is a preacher who often unconsciously picks his nose. It is bad enough when he does so in private conversation; it is disastrous when he does so from the pulpit. For many of us, our distracting mannerisms are not that serious, but they still need to be addressed in order for us to improve our sermon delivery. For instance, putting your hands in your pockets can convey the impression that you are laid back about the matter at hand. So you need to be conscious of that and deal with it. Keep getting your hands out of your pockets each time you realize it until you break the habit. Having a wife who reminds you about your distracting mannerisms can be a great help because other people find it too embarrassing to tell you about them. So if your wife points out your mannerisms that are off-putting, listen to her. She may save your preaching career!

Your Eyes

It is important to maintain eye contact with your hearers as much as possible during your preaching. If you do not give the impression to your congregation that you are looking at them, they soon lose concentration because they assume you are not really interested in them but are absorbed in your own little world. So, as a general rule, look down or at your notes only when you need to do so. As much as possible, look at the people in front of you.

In order to maintain eye contact with your hearers, you need to have an easy outline for your sermon. If your sermon outline is like a virgin jungle, you will need to keep your eyes on the map and compass to avoid getting lost. If it is like a well-planned city, you will easily memorize the turns ahead of you and will enjoy looking at the buildings and the people while you drive to your destination. So make it your goal before considering your sermon preparation done that you can easily tell the skeleton and structure of your sermon without looking at your notes. Let the notes be used more for the details you will need as you preach.

One major advantage with eye contact, apart from arresting wandering minds, is that you get immediate feedback on your sermon. You are preaching in real time. If people do not understand what you are saying, you can see it written all over their faces. This will cause you to further explain your point or to add an illustration that was not originally in your notes. It may even cause you to slow your pace so that you do not leave the people behind. So, if you are naturally shy and thus find it difficult to look at people, you have to overcome that shyness for the sake of effective sermon delivery.

Conclusion

This chapter may sound like a lot of rules about sermon delivery. I hope that is not the way I have come across. Rather, treat this chapter like a checklist. Read it to see where you may have become sloppy in your sermon delivery so that you correct the sloppiness and thus become a more effective preacher. As you do so, you must still work toward forgetting about yourself and concentrating on communicating God's word to your hearers. I began by stating the importance of spending time in prayerfully meditating on your sermon. I cannot emphasize this enough. To go into the pulpit right after spending time in sharing hilarious jokes will not aid you in your preaching. Let the contemplation of the awesome work at hand bring your mind and heart into the right frame as you represent God to a dying world.

Since preaching is an art, you do well to sit at the feet of good preachers often. As you listen to their sermons for the edification of your soul, go one step further and try to see what makes them effective communicators of the word of God. What is it about their sermon delivery that hooks you and keeps you hooked? Whereas you should not simply copy what they do, learn from them and see how you can improve your own sermon delivery. Today's technology enables you to watch videos of the best preachers on the planet without missing preaching in your own pulpit on Sunday. Why not make use of this to improve your preaching?

I have asserted that beyond what you bring into the pulpit from your sermon preparation, sermon delivery is largely about thoughts and emotions conveyed through your voice, gestures, and eyes. These must be natural vehicles of your thoughts and emotions. Your thoughts must inform your emotions, which in turn must inform your voice, gestures, and eyes. Only when this is the case can you preach with integrity and true effectiveness.

Finally, always pray for the help of the Holy Spirit in your preaching. This must be a silent prayer before, during, and after your preaching. Ultimately, the Holy Spirit alone is able to give life to the dead. He regenerates dead souls, and He does so through the instrumentality of the word. This often happens even as you preach. So pray that the Holy Spirit will use your preaching to bring souls into God's kingdom and to build them up in their most holy faith. Pray that He will do far more exceedingly abundantly with your preaching than you are able to ask or even imagine. Pray that the powers of the coming age will be evident in your sermon delivery. Ask for the Holy Spirit, and may He come upon you as you preach.

A story is told of an English-speaking boy who went on vacation with his parents to a non-English-speaking European country. On Sunday the parents tried to find an English-speaking church, but their search proved futile. Finally, they decided to attend a non-English-speaking church, hoping they would understand enough to come away with something. As they were driving back to their residence, the boy tugged at his father's shirt and asked, "Dad, what was the preacher talking about?" The father answered vaguely, but the boy was not satisfied. He asked the father again, "Dad, what was the preacher talking about?" The father's second answer still did not satisfy the boy, and so he asked a third time with even greater intensity and tears in his eyes. When the father noticed the tears he asked his son what the problem was. The boy answered, "Dad, I did not understand a word of what the preacher was saying, but the way he spoke gave me the impression that whatever it was he was speaking about was a matter of life and death!" Oh, that we may all preach like that!

Writings of Steven J. Lawson

Men Who Win: Pursuing the Ultimate Prize. Colorado Springs, Colo.: NavPress, 1992.

When All Hell Breaks Loose, You May Be Doing Something Right: Surprising Insights from the Life of Job. Colorado Springs, Colo.: NavPress, 1993.

Final Call. Wheaton, Ill.: Crossway, 1994.

Faith Under Fire: Standing Strong When Satan Attacks. Wheaton, Ill.: Crossway, 1995.

Heaven Help Us: Truths about Eternity That Will Help You Live Today. Colorado Springs, Colo.: NavPress, 1995.

The Legacy: What Every Father Wants to Leave His Child. Sisters, Ore.: Multnomah, 1998.

Absolutely Sure: Settle the Question of Eternal Life. Sisters, Ore.: Multnomah, 1999.

Made in Our Image: What Shall We Do with a "User-Friendly" God? Sisters, Ore.: Multnomah, 2000.

Famine in the Land: A Passionate Call for Expository Preaching. Chicago: Moody, 2003.

Psalms 1–75. Holman Old Testament Commentary. Nashville, Tenn.: Holman Reference, 2003. Coauthored with Max E. Anders.

Job. Holman Old Testament Commentary. Nashville, Tenn.: Holman Reference, 2004. Coauthored with Max E. Anders.

Foundations of Grace: 1400 BC–AD 100. Lake Mary, Fla.: Reformation Trust, 2006.

Psalms 76–150. Holman Old Testament Commentary. Nashville, Tenn.: Holman Reference, 2006. Coauthored with Max E. Anders.

The Expository Genius of John Calvin. Lake Mary, Fla.: Reformation Trust, 2007.

The Unwavering Resolve of Jonathan Edwards. Orlando, Fla.: Reformation Trust, 2008.

Pillars of Grace: AD 100–1564. Lake Mary, Fla.: Reformation Trust, 2011.

The Gospel Focus of Charles Spurgeon. Orlando, Fla.: Reformation Trust, 2012.

Preaching the Psalms: Unlocking the Unsearchable Riches of David's Treasury. Darlington, U.K.: EP Books, 2012.

The Evangelistic Zeal of George Whitefield. Orlando, Fla.: Reformation Trust, 2013.

The Heroic Boldness of Martin Luther. Orlando, Fla.: Reformation Trust, 2013.

In It to Win It. Eugene, Ore.: Harvest House, 2013.

The Kind of Preaching God Blesses. Eugene, Ore.: Harvest House, 2013.

John Knox: Fearless Faith. Ross-shire, Scotland: Christian Focus, 2014.

The Daring Mission of William Tyndale. Orlando, Fla.: Reformation Trust, 2015.

The Passionate Preaching of Martyn Lloyd-Jones. Orlando, Fla.: Reformation Trust, 2015.

Contributors

Joel R. Beeke is president and professor of systematic theology and homiletics at Puritan Reformed Theological Seminary, a pastor of the Heritage Netherlands Reformed Congregation in Grand Rapids, Michigan, and editorial director of Reformation Heritage Books.

Dustin W. Benge received his MDiv from the Southern Baptist Theological Seminary, Louisville, Kentucky, where he is currently a PhD candidate. He is the editor for *Expositor Magazine* and the director of operations for One Passion Ministries, Dallas, Texas.

Iain D. Campbell is the minister of Point Free Church, a congregation of the Free Church of Scotland on the Isle of Lewis. He is also adjunct professor of church history at Westminster Theological Seminary.

Sinclair B. Ferguson is dean of the doctor of ministry program at Ligonier Academy of Biblical and Theological Studies and a Ligonier Ministries teaching fellow. Prior to moving back to his native land of Scotland, Sinclair served as minister of First Presbyterian Church, Columbia, South Carolina.

W. Robert Godfrey is president and professor of church history at Westminster Theological Seminary in California. He is also a minister in the United Reformed Church and a Ligonier Ministries teaching fellow.

Ian Hamilton is the minister of Cambridge Presbyterian Church in Cambridge, England. He serves on the boards of the Banner of Truth Trust and Greenville Presbyterian Theological Seminary, South Carolina, where he is also an adjunct teacher.

Michael A. G. Haykin is professor of church history and biblical spirituality at the Southern Baptist Theological Seminary, Louisville, Kentucky. He also serves as the director of the Andrew Fuller Center for Baptist Studies at the same institution and as an adjunct professor at Puritan Reformed Theological Seminary in Grand Rapids, Michigan.

John MacArthur is the pastor-teacher of Grace Community Church in Sun Valley, California. He also serves as president of the Master's Seminary and College and is the featured teacher with Grace to You media ministry, which is heard around the world.

Conrad Mbewe is pastor of Kabwata Baptist Church in Lusaka, Zambia, and is widely regarded as the "African Spurgeon." His PhD is in the area of missions. He serves as the principal of Lusaka Ministerial College and the chancellor of the African Christian University in Zambia.

R. Albert Mohler Jr. serves as president of The Southern Baptist Theological Seminary, Louisville, Kentucky. He also serves as professor of Christian theology at Southern Seminary. He is the host of two programs: *The Briefing*, a daily analysis of news and events from a Christian worldview; and *Thinking in Public*, a series of conversations with the day's leading thinkers.

John J. Murray joined the Banner of Truth Trust in London as an assistant editor in 1960. He trained for the gospel ministry at Edinburgh University and at the Free Church College. He served congregations of the Free Church of Scotland in Argyll and Edinburgh. Since retiring he has assisted in several congregations in Glasgow, where he now resides.

R. C. Sproul is founder and chairman of Ligonier Ministries and is featured daily on the radio program *Renewing Your Mind*. He is also chancellor of Reformation Bible College and co-pastor of Saint Andrews Chapel in Sanford, Florida.

Derek W. H. Thomas serves as the minister of preaching and teaching at First Presbyterian Church, Columbia, South Carolina. He is also professor of systematic and pastoral theology at Reformed Theological Seminary in Atlanta, Georgia, and as an adjunct professor at Puritan Reformed Theological Seminary in Grand Rapids, Michigan.

Geoffrey Thomas has served as the pastor of Alfred Place Baptist Church in Aberystwyth, Wales, for over fifty years. He is also visiting professor of historical theology at Puritan Reformed Theological Seminary, Grand Rapids, Michigan.